55BKR J32   8367 B5Q

TURENNE DES PRÉS, François. *Children of Yayoute: Folk Tales of Haiti.* illus. by author. 96p. CIP. Universe. 1994.

Tr $19.95. ISBN 0-87663-791-8. LC 93-50605.

Gr 4-7—A collection of 12 Haitian folktales, written by the late Haitian artist/writer. Some relate historical anecdotes and provide insight into local customs, while others reflect their African origins. The selections are clearly written and beautifully illustrated with full-color plates of Turenne des Prés's vibrant oil paintings and watercolors. These stories impart the rich cultural heritage of the people of African descent who, as a result of diaspora, found themselves in this region. A glossary of indigenous terms and sayings is provided.—*Barbara Osborne Williams, Queens Borough Public*

CHILDREN OF YAYOUTE

FOLK TALES OF HAITI

CHILDREN OF YAYOUTE

FOLK TALES OF HAITI

FRANÇOIS
TURENNE DES PRÉS

CALIFORNIA AFRO-AMERICAN
MUSEUM FOUNDATION, LOS ANGELES

UNIVERSE PUBLISHING,
NEW YORK

Haiti, whose name is derived from the Arawak Indian word meaning "high ground," is the oldest black republic in the world and the second oldest independent nation in the western hemisphere. It occupies the western third of the Caribbean island of Hispaniola, which it shares with the Dominican Republic. Haiti lies between the islands of Cuba and Puerto Rico in the Caribbean Sea.

Most of the people are descendants of African slaves brought to the island in great numbers in the early 1700s to work the coffee and spice plantations of the French colonists. Most speak a language called Haitian Creole, partly based on French. Many still follow some of the customs their ancestors brought from Africa. One of the most often cited examples of the pattern is in their religious practices. While the majority of Haitians consider themselves Roman Catholic, many practice a combination of Christian and African ritual referred to as "voodoo." It is largely due to voodooism that Haiti has been known as the "land of mystery."

First published in the
United States of America in 1994
by Universe Publishing
300 Park Avenue South
New York, NY 10010

© 1993 The Trust of François Turenne des Prés

The following stories: How Malice Went to Learn
a Trade, The King's Cherished Lamb, How Malice
Sent the Donkey to Marry the King, and How Bouqui
Was Thrown Over the Cliff © 1949 by François Marcel
Turenne des Prés, originally published in *Children of
Yayoute: Folk Tales of Haiti* in 1949 by Editions Henri
Deschamps, Port-au-Prince, Haiti.

94 95 96 97 98 99 / 10 9 8 7 6 5 4 3 2 1

Printed in Singapore

Library of Congress Cataloging-in-Publication Data

Turenne des Prés, 1907-1990.
      Children of yayoute : folk tales of Haiti / François Turenne des Prés.
        p. cm.
      Published in association with the California Afro-American Museum, Los Angeles.
      Summary: A collection of Haitian folk tales featuring magical human and animal characters,
from tricksters and buffoons to dancing dolls and talking fish.
      ISBN 0-87663-791-8
      1. Tales—Haiti. [1. Folklore—Haiti.] I. California Afro-American Museum. II. Title.
PZ8.1.T7495Ch 1994
[398.2]—dc20   93-50605
                                                         CIP
                                                         AC

Edited for CAAM Foundation by Aurelia Brooks and Nancy Mc Kinney
Designed by Christina Bliss

On the title page:
François Turenne des Prés (1907–1990), *Le Marche Haitien
(Haitian Market)*, watercolor on paper, 21 x 29 in.,
Collection of Chantal Turenne des Prés

Contents

Jeu sur le Chemin (Game on the Path)

INTRODUCTION

Josquin des Prés, son of the late Haitian artist/writer François Turenne des Prés, approached me in early 1991 to assist his family in having a volume of François's Haitian folktales, *Children of Yayoute* (Children of African Ancestry), re-published, I was both intrigued and excited. The California Afro-American Museum Foundation had published several successful exhibition catalogues, but never a book.

What made the idea even more appealing was the family's wish to include paintings of the senior Turenne des Prés to illustrate the stories, several pieces of which are in the Foundation's collection of fine art. The idea of sharing these works with a wider audience, particularly young people, in such a unique context could not be resisted.

Nancy McKinney, the Museum's Associate Editor of Publications, was delighted with the prospect of joining the art and folklore of Haiti under one cover. As good fortune would have it, Nancy located an interested publisher, Universe Books, and the project moved closer to reality.

Later during discussions with the Turenne des Prés family, the existence of an unpublished manuscript of Haitian folktales recorded by François was revealed. "The Tales of Ma Bonne" (good nursemaid) proved to be different yet equally captivating and opened up another dimension of stories recounted in parts of Haiti by nursemaids entertaining their young charges. Young François was one of those children. In later years, François explained that his particular Ma Bonne had been a nursemaid to a well-traveled family and had no doubt gathered stories from Europe and retold them in her own Haitian style. She also created many of her stories, including in them historical anecdotes and local Haitian customs.

The more traditional stories, whose origins are African, feature the exploits of two creatures, one called Malice, the clever trickster, and the other Bouqui, who was usually on the losing end of most adventures. Just as with similar characters in African folklore, it is not known whether they are people or animals, so they may change from one story to another.

François felt that his San Naa (grandmother), Madame Rosana Pierre-Louis, was the greatest interpreter of Malice and Bouqui stories of all time. In telling these stories, San Naa followed the traditional pattern of storytelling, as do all Haitians even to this day.

Standing under the open starlit sky, with the audience in a semi-circle, sitting on logs, the ground, chairs or upturned wooden mortars, she would say with a snap

"Cric?"

"Crac!" the audience would reply, also with a snap.

"Time-time?" (pronounced team-team) she would snap to get their attention.

"Bois sec!" (pronounced bwa sok, which means dry wood) the audience would reply, meaning that they wanted to hear the stories.

"How many branches? (how many stories?)" she would ask.

"Twelve branches! (twelve stories!)" the audience wanted to hear that evening.

"Bon!" she would reply agreeably.

And so we begin with a mix of both volumes in this edition of *Children of Yayoute*. We hope you enjoy these stories and the art of François Turenne des Prés as much as we have enjoyed bringing them to you.

Aurelia Brooks,
Chief Executive Officer
CAAM Foundation

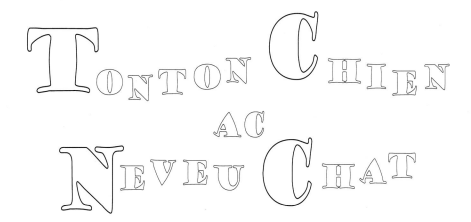

Tonton Chien ac Neveu Chat

Cric? Crac! There was once a cat and a dog who were very good friends. They lived together in the same house as though they were relatives. The cat called the dog Uncle and the dog called the cat Nephew, so close were they to one another.

One day, Tonton Chien (uncle dog) and Neveu Chat (nephew cat) went to town together. In the marketplace, they bought a pot of butter with money they had received for cutting sugarcane in the fields. Tonton Chien carried the pot of butter home on his head while his nephew trotted uphill behind him. When they arrived at their sugarcane leaf thatched hut, Tonton Chien took a fresh clean piece of banana leaf and covered the pot of butter. He placed it in a big earthen jar of water in a corner of the house. He suggested that they should feast on it only on special days. Sunday was the best day, because God made it a day of rest, and all God's children ate the best of everything on Sunday.

The next morning being a weekday, Thursday, they rose early. Neveu Chat passed near the pot of butter, wriggling his whiskers and sniffing the air.

Tonton Chien lit his clay pipe and took up his hoe. Neveu Chat also lit his clay pipe and took up his machete and stuck it in his belt. They headed for the field to weed their patch of sweet potatoes.

When they arrived in the field, Tonton Chien began to till the stony red earth with all his might at one end and Neveu Chat swung his machete, weeding lazily at another end, while smoke from their pipes went up like smoke from two little boats.

When the sun began to get hot, Neveu Chat suddenly put his machete in his belt and took the pipe from between his teeth. "Oh, I forgot!" he said.

Une Case dans la Brousse (A Hut in the Jungle)

"...Forgot what?" inquired the dog, after he had taken the pipe out of his mouth.

"A friend has asked me to be the godfather of his child. I should have been there long ago."

"Go right ahead," said Tonton Chien. "I don't mind working for both of us."

The cat went directly to the hut, removed the banana leaf from the pot of butter, and ate to his heart's content. Then he covered it up again, placed it in the big earthen jar, and went swiftly back to the field.

"You certainly stayed away a long time," said Tonton Chien when Neveu Chat rejoined him.

"Ah!" sighed Nephew Cat. "I just had to be late because the *marraine* (godmother) was late coming. You know, without a godmother there can be no christening."

"That's all right," said Tonton Chien agreeably. "What is your godchild, a boy or a girl?"

"... A girl, and I am very proud of her."

"I, too, am as proud as I can be. What's her name?" Tonton Chien asked.

"Entamé (well begun) she is called."

"My! that's an unusual name," Tonton Chien remarked.

The cat raised his back proudly and agreed.

They worked a while longer. When the sun was too hot they went home.

The next day they were working in the field again. When the sun was half way in the sky, Neveu Chat dropped his hoe. "*Ma cousine* is calling me. I can hear her yelling at the top of her voice. Can't you?" he asked Tonton Chien, who was raking dead weeds from the potato patch.

"No, I can't," he said, "I only hear the chickens cackling. They always cackle like that at noontime, especially when the sun is hot."

"I forgot that I had promised to be the godfather of her child. It must be the reason she is calling me. That's no chicken cackling," he said.

Conte Vaudouesque (Voodoo Story) (detail)

"Well, if that's the case, you had better go right ahead. Don't let me keep you," said Tonton Chien. "I'll work for both of us."

Neveu Chat kicked his working tools aside and ran directly to the hut. He ate his stomach full of butter and then ran back to join Tonton Chien, who had been working so hard that sweat trickled down his back.

"There you are!" exclaimed Tonton Chien, resting his chin on the end of his hoe. That was the first time he had stopped working since Neveu Chat had left him. "You stayed long enough again. The godmother must have been late for the christening?"

Carnaval Haitien (Haitian Carnival) (detail)

"No," replied Neveu Chat, licking his paw which got into the butter while he was in the pot. "The christening was very formal this time. The priest took longer to do this christening, that's why. Each priest does it in his own way, you know."

"Those things will happen," agreed Tonton Chien. "What is this one, boy or girl, and what's the name?"

"It's a boy this time and his name is Mi-Mangé (half gone). He is even cuter than the first one," added Neveu Chat.

"...A strange and unusual name you gave this one, too," Tonton Chien remarked. "But it must be all right."

They worked awhile and, when the sun was too hot, Uncle Dog put his hoe over his shoulder and Nephew Cat put his machete in his belt and they went home.

The next morning they went into the field again, but before Neveu Chat had cut half a dozen green twigs with his machete he said, "Ah, no! It can't be!"

"...What can't be?" asked Tonton Chien.

"Someone's calling me again. This time I'm not going. It is not fair to let you do all the hard work all the time."

"I must be getting deaf," said Tonton Chien, trying to listen, "because I only hear a calf mooing in the field yonder."

"Well," said Neveu Chat, his hand in the pocket of his blue denim trousers and twisting his paw in the red earth, "I can hear the voice. It must be someone who wants me to stand as godfather again. They just won't leave me alone. 'Cat do this! Cat do that! Cat be my child's godfather' is all I hear wherever I turn," he said. "But I want to stay and help you. Whoever wants me as godfather may just as well be angry with me, because I'm not going."

"Don't let your friends get angry with you. Go right ahead and be a godfather. A third time won't hurt," said Tonton Chien generously.

So Neveu Chat stuck his machete in his belt and went right to the hut and ate what was left of the butter. Then he covered the pot and left it as if no one had ever touched it. He came back as quickly as his feet could carry him, licking the butter from his jaws.

"What kept you so long this time?" asked Tonton Chien.

"The godchild was larger, harder to handle. It took two priests, instead of the usual one, to do the christening," answered Neveu Chat.

"My, it must be nice to be the godfather of such fine children," said Tonton Chien, nodding approvingly.

"Nice is not the word. Wonderful is the word. Just wonderful! And I'm proud of every one of my godchildren. But I enjoyed the christenings above all."

"By the way what did you call this one?" asked Tonton Chien.

"Tout-Fini (all gone), even though it is a girl," said Neveu Chat.

Tonton Chien chuckled. He had to put one of his front paws over his jaw to keep Neveu Chat from seeing how he was laughing at his expense. "Your godchildren certainly have unusual names indeed. But it must be all right."

Then Tonton Chien showed the cat the pile of sweet potatoes he had dug for their Sunday dinner. Together they put them in their *halfor* (straw bag) and took them home.

The next morning was Sunday and Tonton Chien built a fire and put the sweet potatoes on to cook. Then he laid the table with freshly cut banana leaves. When the sweet potatoes were done, he dished them into a large *coui* (eating gourd), put them on the table, and went after the pot of butter.

All the while Neveu Cat kept watching him from the corner of his eye. Lo! the pot of butter was so light that the dog couldn't believe it was the same pot he had put in the big earthen jar days before.

"Oh-oh, *mes amis*!" Tonton Chien shouted when he looked in. "The pot is empty!"

He thought it over but could not understand what had happened. He rubbed the inside of the pot with his paw, but the paw came out clean and didn't even smell of butter.

While Tonton Chien was trying to figure out what had happened to the butter, Neveu Chat went under the bed to hide. He knew that Tonton Chein would soon realize what had happened to the butter.

Tonton Chien was still puzzled. He scratched the back of his head, trying to think.

Suddenly he said, "Now I know why you named your three godchildren, Entamé, Mi-Mangé, Tout-Fini." He threw back his head and barked angrily. "We are going to settle this! Entamé, Mi-Mangé, and Tout-Fini, indeed!"

He reached under the bed to get the cat, but Neveu Chat scratched his nose and said, "I don't see why you get yourself so upset and blame me because of a naughty pot. It was the heat which melted the butter and it evaporated into the air and left the pot clean. If you don't believe me, ask that fellow who has just passed behind the house."

Tonton Chien ran to see who had just passed behind the house. Sly Neveu Chat took the occasion to run outside and climb a big tree where he was out of the dog's reach.

Because of this deceit and trickery, the dogs of Haiti to this day hold a grudge against cats.

And the cats know this, and therefore always sleep with one eye closed and one eye open, watching out for the dogs.

Chanson pour une Demi-déesse Blessèe
(Song for a Wounded semi-goddess)

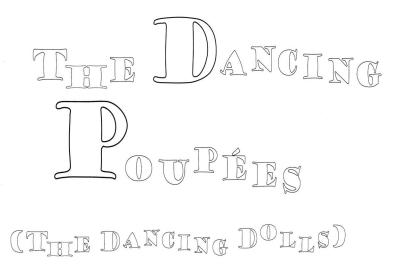

THE DANCING POUPÉES

(THE DANCING DOLLS)

Near the forest of Fond Cochon lived a farmer named Frê André with his wife Sô Amédée and their little daughter named Louise. Several years before Louise was born, they had also a girl and a boy named Boubie and Jocelin.

One day Frê André and his wife sent the two children into the forest to gather wild mushrooms, but they never returned and no one saw them again. The poor parents and all their neighbors searched the forest from end to end, but the children could not be found. Since then Sô Amédée had been sad and unhappy. Her grief made her cross and snappish to her husband and little Louise.

One New Year's Day, Frê André came home and asked his wife, "Where is our dinner, good wife? I am hungry."

Sô Amédée laughed and said, "Dinner, do you say? Where would I get it from? Remember, my good man, that ever since our dear children disappeared in the forest you have never worked to bring any money home. Go sit in the corner, *mon cher*."

Louise looked sadly at her mother, then ran to her father and said, "Leave papa alone, maman. Today is the New Year. Let him be happy. All of us must make merry with the little we have."

Frê André held her tightly against him and said, "That's my good girl. She looks out for me, and I have a present for her, too." He pulled two small wooden dolls out of his pocket and gave them to Louise.

"Oh, papa!" Louise exclaimed. "You make me very happy on New Year's Day!"

"It would be better if you got her some food to eat and some clothes to wear," said the good wife. "It hurts me to the very core of my heart. This morning I looked at all the children of the neighborhood, wearing their new clothes, calling at every house, wishing everybody *Une Heureuse Année* (Happy New Year); merrily drinking sodas colored in green, in pink, or in red, and sweet wines; eating cornstarch cookies and *rapadou* offered to them; and here, our little Louise in a dress so tattered, so covered with all different colored patches on it, was too shabby to take part in all this."

"The *poupées* (dolls) are very nice, and I like them very much, maman," said Louise.

"If I had my way," said Sô Amédée, "I would burn these silly dolls in the fire. Where did you get them from, if I may ask?"

"Don't you dare burn her dolls!" said Frê André. "If you must know where I got them from, let me tell you that as I was passing by the place near the forest where our two children went to pick wild mushrooms and never returned, I heard a voice which said,

    " 'Pick us up!

    Pick us up!

    We have no hut!' "

"I imagined it was a sound made by the wind, so I walked on. But the voice said again,

    " 'Pick us up!

    Pick us up!

    We have no hut!' "

"So I turned around, looked here and there and saw no one; but then I saw these two little wooden dolls lying on a big rock in the hot sun. They looked almost as if they were alive, so I picked them up and brought them home to Louise. Now that I have told you all you wanted to know, you should be pleased and say no more," concluded the farmer.

"All that is a *Nonc Bouqui and Ti-Malice* tale, and just plain nonsense," said she angrily, "if our kind neighbors had not brought us some *doucounou* (corn meal cake) and a small bottle of liquor, we'd have had to eat pumpkin soup at all three meals this New Year's Day."

"What's wrong with pumpkin soup?" said he. "It's our national dish. Everybody, rich and poor, eats it all through the holidays. In addition to the big ripe pumpkin I brought, it has in it some cabbage leaves, celery stalks, cloves and black peppers. It also has a few strings of vermicelli, a pinch of rice, a few pieces of bread floating on the top of it, as well as those beef bones I brought. What more do you want for a meal on this Independence Day?..."

"Ugh!" grunted Sô Amédée, shrugging her shoulders, before Frê André had even finished speaking.

"Don't interrupt me, *ma chère*, when I am talking," said Frê André. "The soup is magic," he continued. "It's good for whatever ails you. Why, that soup is a wonder. More than that I've heard that this soup has cured many people in the mountains of their ailments, quicker than any leaf from the medicine man. The only thing it has not done yet is to bring the dead back to life. I think you had better go sit in the corner, wife."

Sô Amédée took a couple of whiffs from her red-clay pipe, then said, "Yes, but those beef bones of yours were so old, and they smelled so bad that I thought I'd have to soak them in *lait de chaux* (limewater) before using them."

"Aha!" Frê André breathed sarcastically. "You didn't soak them in *lait de chaux* before using them, which is the reason why the soup has a much better flavor than all that high seasoning of yours could give it."

"Ugh!" she said. "Go sit in the corner, papa." Then from her old pipe she puffed white smoke into the air.

She put wood under her *chaudière* (iron kettle), lit the fire, and heated the soup. When it was good and hot, she gave a portion to Louise, one to the farmer, and took one herself. All began to sip from their *couis*. They were so poor that they had no spoons or plates.

Louise sipped and said, "This soup is magic, papa says, so I shall feed it to my dolls."

"Stop that nonsense, child," said Sô Amédée.

"Let the child alone, for she has to play," said the father.

And so Louise went on sipping her soup, and each time she sipped she dipped her finger in the *coui* and rubbed some soup on the dolls' mouths.

When they had finished their soup, they opened the banana leaf which wrapped the *doucounou*. Louise laid her dolls on the bed so that her hands could be freer to eat her *doucounou*.

Then the most surprising thing in the world happened.

One of the dolls sat up, jumped down from the bed, and began to dance; and then the other began to dance too. Frê André, Sô Amédée and Louise were amazed.

They called in all their neighbors to see the great miracle. The farmer's one-room hut was full of people, and they made a circle to watch the dancing dolls. The dolls danced and danced and all the time their knees sounded Click, Clack! Click, Clack! Click, Clack! Soon they began to waver like mechanical dolls that needed to be rewound. They could dance no more. First, one fell on the earthen floor, and then the other fell down, too.

All the people were alarmed and exclaimed:

"Oh, *mon Dieu*! the poor little dolls! What has happened to them?"

Little Louise exclaimed, "But look! They are breathing!"

And indeed the little dolls were breathing, and suddenly before all the crowd they grew to human size. Soon both of them stood up and began to talk. They were human children, a boy and a girl.

Paysage Haitien
(Haitian Scene)
(detail)

18

"Maman!" said one.

"Papa!" said the other.

"Don't you know us?" both said together.

They were the farmer's children who had been lost in the forest so long before. A *loup-garou* (werewolf) had put a spell on them and laid them upon a rock in the hot sun so that when they were well dried he could cook them into *calalou* (stew).

After Boubie and Jocelin had finished their tales, Frê André said to his wife, "Good wife, the pumpkin soup that Louise gave them had salt in it, and no magic spell can withstand salt. That's what took the *loup-garou's* spell away!"

Sô Amédée wept for joy, because she was so happy to have her children back with her again. And she said to Frê André as she wept, "Frê André, I will never tell you to sit in the corner again!"

And it is because of this miracle that pumpkin soup has remained the most important New Year's dish in Haiti.

Chanson pour une Demi-déesse Blessèe (Song for a Wounded semi-goddess) (detail)

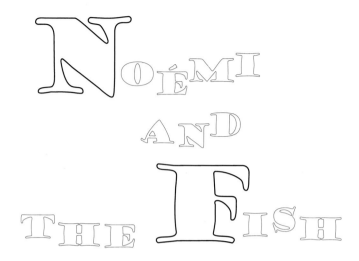

NOÉMI AND THE FISH

Among the green trees on a hilltop there was a little thatched cottage. In it lived a family of four, a mother and a father, a lonely little girl called Noémi, and Ti-Frê, her little brother.

Below the hill, a river as blue as the sky wound across the land into the valley.

There was something mysterious about the river. From afar it always looked beautiful and blue, but close at hand it was reddish and muddy in color. There was no other water around, so all the people in that section of Haiti had to use the muddy water even though they did not like to.

One day Noémi's mother sent her with a *calabash* (drinking gourd) to fetch water. When the girl arrived at the river, it was muddier than ever and full of dry leaves. She stepped over to a rock and began to clear away the leaves with her hand, when her little gold ring slipped off her finger and sank into the muddy stream.

Noémi was very sad, because her godmother had given her this ring and she cherished it greatly. She sat down on the rock and began to cry. The tears ran down her cheeks and fell into the river. At once, the spot where the tears fell became clear. Noémi was surprised to be able to see deep down into the stream. In the bottom she saw her ring, but it looked as large as a barrel hoop.

She continued to cry so hard that the water became foamy and she could no longer see through it. Suddenly, between a wave and the foam, a fish came to the top. He was a very beautiful fish and he could speak.

"Why are you crying, *ma petite?*" he asked her.

"My...my ring is in the water...my pretty little ring..." she said between sobs.

"Do not cry," the fish said to her. "I will get your ring for you. But you must promise to do something for me in return."

"Anything. Anything!" she said.

"When you come to get water, will you call me and talk to me a little while? I am so lonely in the water. I'll fill your *calabash* with very clear water for you each time," he said.

"I will be glad to call you and talk to you, but I don't know your name," Noémi answered.

"My name is Thézin and I live in the stream," replied the fish. "I'll teach you a little song to sing each time you come. When I hear it, I'll come up. But you must always come alone and no one else must know this song."

And he sang:

"Zin, zin, Thézin! Oh, *zammi mouin,*
Where are you? Zin, zin, zin, zin!
Thézin in the muddy stream!"

After Noémi had told Thézin her name and learned the song, the fish dove down into the stream and brought the ring up to her. Then he took her *calabash* in his two fins and swam away. When he came back, it was filled with water as clear as pure air.

"Thank you, Thézin, *cher ami.* I'll see you tomorrow." And she walked away toward the hills.

Thézin swam back into the stream.

On her way home, Noémi repeated the little song over and over so she wouldn't forget it. Now she had found a friend with whom she could talk each time she went to fetch water.

The next day when she was sent after water, she ran as fast as though she had wings. When she reached the river's edge, she sang her song:

"Zin, zin, Thézin! Oh, *zammi mouin,*
Where are you? Zin, zin, zin, zin!
Thézin in the muddy stream!"

The water bubbled and the fish splashed up to the surface.

Félicité

Every day, and sometimes twice a day, Thézin and Noémi talked a long time. Noémi was happier than she had ever been in all her life. Her friendship with Thézin grew stronger each time they met.

Life among the green hills was no longer dull.

At home her mother was puzzled when she saw how the girl had changed. She wondered how it came about that the water Noémi brought home was so clear. But Noémi wouldn't tell anyone.

One morning when Noémi was sent for water, Ti-Frê followed her secretly. He hid among the reeds and heard his sister singing the strange tune. Then, the water gurgled and the beautiful fish came up. Noémi and Thézin had their friendly talk, after which Thézin took the *calabash*, swam away, and brought it back filled with fresh water.

The song was so strange that the boy could not forget it. He sang it all the way home.

When he came home, Ti-Frê told his mother that he now knew how to get clear water.

"It is Thézin who gets the water for Ti-So," he said.

"Who is Thézin?"

Ti-Frê told his mother all about the fish and the song he had heard his sister sing. He sang it to her. The tune was so enchanting that she too kept on singing it until she knew it by heart. She told her husband about it and sang the song for him. He, too, found the tune very bewitching.

Finally both agreed that the creature Ti-Frê had seen entertaining Noémi must have been an underwater *loa* (god).

They were afraid for Noémi, since it might be a mischievous god.

On the other hand, if Thézin were merely a fish, so splendid a catch would be worth having. Either way, they had to know more.

The next morning, in order to get her out of the way, Noémi's mother gave the girl the donkey laden with vegetables to sell in the marketplace.

They had planned to go to the river while Noémi was gone and catch the fish for dinner.

But on her way to town, Noémi stopped by the river as usual to see Thézin. She sang the song and Thézin came up to her. For the first time since she had known him, he was very gloomy.

"*Qu'est-ce-qu'il y a?* Why are you so sad, Thézin?"

"There is bad news, *ma petit amie*. Some calamity is going to happen."

"Oh, what can it be?" Noémi asked anxiously.

"You are going to town," Thézin said. "When the sun is half way up to the sky, look in your handkerchief. If you see a drop of blood, come back to the river quickly because I will want to see you once more."

Oh, Mauvaise Augure! (Omen!)

23

"Are you going away?" Noémi asked, weeping.

"Do not weep so, *ma chère*. What is to happen will happen. And we will see each other again."

They talked a long time and though they hated to part, Noémi finally sprang on the donkey's back and rode toward the city.

Thézin swam away under the stream.

After Noémi had left for the marketplace, Ti-Frê led his parents to the spot. When they arrived there, the father sang the song in a deep bass.

But the fish did not come up.

Then the mother sang in her soprano voice, not so sweet and young as the voice of Noémi.

The fish did not come up.

Now Ti-Frê tried his little silver bell-like voice, which was very much like that of Noémi's.

"Zin, zin, Thézin! Oh, *zammi mouin*,

Where are you? Zin, zin, zin, zin!

Thézin in the muddy stream!"

At once the water bubbled and became very clear.

Thézin came splashing to the surface.

Noémi's father swung his well-sharpened *machete* and cut off the fish's head and dragged him out of the water.

When they reached home with the fish, they cooked enough for dinner, leaving an eating gourd full for Noémi, and the rest was laid out on the thatched roof to dry.

While they were eating the fish at home, Noémi, in the marketplace, had not yet sold all her vegetables. But when the church bell struck twelve, she looked up in the sky and saw the sun was half way up. She quickly pulled out her small handkerchief.

"Oh, Thézin!" was all she could gasp out, for she saw the drop of blood in it. In her sorrow the little girl was utterly devastated.

She took her donkey and threw the harness on him, then jumped on his back, leaving all her vegetables in the marketplace.

Everybody said, "There goes a mad girl!"

But Noémi did not hear them. Her mind was only on Thézin in the deep stream. She beat the donkey right and left with a piece of rope to hurry him uphill. When she arrived at the river's edge, she jumped from the donkey's back and ran to the usual spot.

"Zin, zin, Thézin! Oh, *zammi mouin,*
Where are you? Zin, zin, zin, zin!
Thézin in the muddy stream!" she sang.

But no Thézin came. The water bubbled red.

She sang several times as she wept, and after each verse the water bubbled red, but Thézin never came up.

Noémi spent the whole afternoon, sitting on the rock by the river, weeping and singing.

When the sun sank behind the mountain, she went sadly home. When she arrived her parents and her brother were not there, but she saw a huge fish drying on the roof. Inside the cottage she saw a gourd of cooked fish left for her. Her heart was broken. She knew what had happened to Thézin. She went outside and sat in her little chair singing as she wept. The tears ran down her cheeks and onto the ground. The tears began to moisten the earth when, mysteriously, the little chair began to sink into the soft earth, as she continued to sing and weep.

Ti-Frê, arriving home from the field saw his sister up to her neck in the ground.

In terror the lad called, "Noémi! *Ça où fait là?* What are you doing there?"

But in her grief, she did not hear him.

Horror stricken, Ti-Frê ran back to the field to get his parents.

When the parents arrived, only one lock of Noémi's hair was seen outside of the earth, but that too was disappearing. The father seized it and, after a mighty pull, the lock of hair remained in his hand, but Noémi sank down under the earth to meet the spirit of Thézin.

Ti-Frê never believed that she was dead because he now realized that Thézin was a god and had taken Noémi to live with him forever in the stream.

Sometimes Ti-Frê would go there and sing.

"Zin, zin, Thézin! Oh, *zammi mouin,*
Where are you? Zin, zin, zin, zin!
Thézin in the muddy stream!" he sang.

But neither Thézin nor Noémi ever appeared and have not to this day been seen.

Paysage Tropical
(Tropical Landscape)

Bien-Aimé and the Magic Orange Tree

There was once a widower, a poor fisherman named Delpée, who had five children. The youngest was a boy called Bien-Aimé.

Their cruel stepmother, Dédé, was not good to the children. Delpée was a man of little courage who was always afraid to interfere when his wife mistreated the children.

One day Dédé went to town and left the children without a bite to eat. She had some oranges on the table, but before leaving she warned them not to touch the fruit or she would punish them.

Several hours after she left, Bien-Aimé began to feel so famished that he was willing to eat the oranges even though he knew his stepmother would beat him terribly. He ate some and encouraged the other children to eat them with him.

Later in the evening, Dédé returned home and found her oranges gone. She was indeed furious. She took her guava switches and whipped the children and sent them to bed without supper. Bien-Aimé, however, did not stay to get a whipping like the others. He ran directly to the cemetery and dropped in a heap on his mother's grave. There he wept and wept until he fell asleep.

When he awoke it was daylight. He still had tears in his eyes, but when he stood

27

up, an orange seed, which had stuck to his blue denim shirt, fell on the grave. Immediately, the seed sprouted into a tiny tree with two small green leaves. When the lad saw that, he sang in a sad voice,

"Grow, orange tree, grow,
And look at the tears in my eyes;
O, orange tree, grow."

The orange tree grew to a full-size tree. The lad was amazed and continued to sing,

"Blossom, orange tree, blossom,
And look at the tears in my eyes;
O, orange tree, blossom,"

Before his weeping eyes, the orange tree was covered with white blossoms, which quickly turned into tiny green oranges.

The lad sang on,

"Grow, orange tree, grow,
And look at the tears in my eyes;
O, orange tree, grow."

And the oranges quickly grew as large as grapefruit.

The lad continued to sing his song.

"Ripen, oranges, ripen,
And look at the tears in my eyes;
O, oranges, ripen."

And all the oranges ripened into the prettiest golden fruit.

Now Bien-Aimé would have liked to pick some of the oranges, but the branches were too high for him to reach. So he sang again,

"Lower your branches, orange tree,
And look at the tears in my eyes;
O, orange tree, lower your branches."

The tree lowered its branches gently to the boy.

He picked some of the golden oranges and ate them. They were juicy and as sweet as though they had been sweetened with honey. After he had eaten to his heart's content, he filled his straw hat with the prettiest oranges he could find on the tree. When he returned home, he found Dédé standing in the doorway, waiting for him.

"*Méchant p'tit garçon* (bad little boy)," she cried, holding her guava switches behind her back, "where have you been all night?" But upon seeing the beautiful oranges, she grinned and said, "Where did you find those oranges?"

"I brought them for you," said Bien-Aimé, "to replace those that I ate yesterday."

Dédé dropped her switches and grabbed the boy's hat. She ate one of the oranges. It was so delicious and sweet that she devoured the rest in no time.

"Show me the tree from which you picked them," she said.

Bien-Aimé hesitated for a moment, but when he saw her moving the guava switches, he led the way to the cemetery. When they got there, Dédé was amazed at the size of the golden oranges on the tree. She plucked one and ate it. Then she reached up to pluck another one but, before she could do so, the boy sang his song.

"Rise high, orange tree, rise high,
And look at the tears in my eyes;
O, orange tree, rise high!"

And the tree rose up high in the air, out of Dédé's reach. Then she changed her sharp tone and said tenderly,

"*Au nom de Dieu* (In the name of God), my child, sing your song so I can have some of those sweet oranges."

"Lower down, orange tree, lower down,
And look at the tears in my eye;
O, orange tree, lower down," sang Bien-Aimé.

The tree lowered itself down. Dédé quickly climbed up and grabbed orange after orange and ate until her stomach was as hard as a tight voodoo drum. When she could not eat anymore, she climbed down.

Now she tried every way she could to think of to make the boy tell her the secret of the orange tree, but he refused. So, she took her switches and started to go after him. But Bien-Aimé quickly climbed up the tree and she after him. When the boy saw that she was way up to the top, he jumped down. Before she had time to jump down too, the boy sang his song,

"Rise high, orange tree, rise high,
And look at the tears in my eyes;
O, orange tree, rise high!"

And the orange tree rose high up into the clouds. When it was high enough Bien-Aimé sang his song,

"Break down, orange tree, break down,
for I have tears in my eyes;
O, orange tree, break down."

And with Dédé on it, the orange tree crashed to the earth!

Bien-Aimé went back home and found his brothers and sisters crying because they were so hungry. He told them about the orange tree and they went to the cemetery. He sang the orange tree to life again and they all ate oranges to their heart's content and went home very happy.

When Delpée returned from his day's fishing and learned what had happened, he rejoiced that the wicked Dédé could no longer mistreat the little ones.

He and his children lived happily together. They were never hungry anymore, but sometimes Bien-Aimé would lead the children to the cemetery to eat the mysterious golden oranges.

But before leaving the cemetery, he never failed to hide his tree in the clouds. That's the reason why, if you should pass by this cemetery, you would not see the orange tree, for it is hidden high up in the clouds.

Félicité (detail)

Opposite page:
Fille avec Fruits sur la Tête
(Girl with Fruit on her Head)

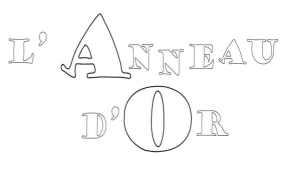

L'Anneau d'Or
(The Golden Ring)

There was once a king who had an only daughter named Princess Zézette, who was still a little girl when her mother was taken ill.

One day the queen called the princess to her bedside.

"Zézette, *ma chère enfant,*" she said, "I shall not be with you very long. I'm going on a far journey and will never come back."

From under her pillow, she pulled a small locket and in it was a golden ring.

"Let me put this ring on your finger. It will protect you against all the wickedness on this wicked island. But whatever you do, you must never part with it for even a second."

With that, the queen gave Zézette her blessing and closed her eyes forever.

Now this ring had a mysterious charm attached to it. If Zézette were to part with it, she would die within forty-eight hours, unless it were put back on her finger within that time. The king knew this, but did not tell his daughter. He simply watched her very carefully to be sure that she did not lose the ring.

Well, many years went by. Zézette grew up and was so beautiful that people traveled from distant islands just to get a glimpse of her. Why, when she went out of doors by day, even the sun would come out from under the clouds just to smile upon her and so would the moon by night.

Her father, the king, grew to love her so much that he couldn't bear to have her out of his sight for even the shortest time. So much was the princess to his life that she could go for a walk in her garden only when the king took his afternoon nap.

But she couldn't go alone. No, indeed! That was too much of a chance to take.

Her nurse must always be with her.

But one afternoon while the king was asleep and her nurse was nowhere around, Princess Zézette went all alone for a walk in the garden, which was near the forest.

Now, in this forest lived a beast. No one knew what sort of beast it was because, up to that moment, no one had ever seen it. Some people said that it was not a beast, but a wicked *loup-garou*. Others said that it was a dragon. But the only thing everyone knew for sure was that there must be something frightful there.

All of a sudden, the beast appeared and started after Princess Zézette.

She did not scream, because in those days it was not considered proper for fine ladies to do such a thing. So, the only thing the princess could do was to run as fast as she could. She picked up a big stone as she ran and threw it at the beast. But he swallowed it in one gulp. She kept on throwing stones until she found no more, but the beast swallowed every one as fast as she could throw them.

When there were no more stones for her to throw, she began to throw her adornments at him. First she threw her crown full of diamonds, but the creature swallowed it. Then she kicked off her little slippers all embroidered with diamonds, and the beast swallowed them too.

Finally, in her fright, she threw him her ring.

My, my!

Poor Zézette!

Apparently the ring was what the creature wanted, for after he had swallowed it, he stopped, and went back to his cave in the forest.

Zézette continued to run until she reached her father's palace. She was in a state of despair.

The king, still half asleep, sprang up. Seeing her in such terror, he caught her in his arms and asked, "*Qu'est ce qu'il y a, ma chère enfant?* What has happened to you?"

Princess Zézette was so out of breath that she could scarcely say a word.

But finally she gasped out all that had happened and fainted right into the king's arms.

He laid her upon her bed, called her nurse, and then sent for the best physicians on the island.

He spread the news of the ring's loss and announced that any man who was

Nue—L'Haitienne (Haitian Nude) (detail)

brave enough to slay this beast and restore his daughter's ring might have her as his bride—and be made a real prince besides. However, the ring must be restored within forty-eight hours or Zézette would die.

Physician after physician came, but each gave up the case. There was no medical treatment that could do the princess any good.

In the meantime, the news of His Majesty's offer echoed everywhere, and all the brave lads came from everywhere and went into the forest to kill the horrid beast. But it was to no avail because the savage creature destroyed every one of them.

Those whom he didn't snap up with his great jaws, he struck with his long scaly tail, and they died.

When the king and his people heard how badly things were going, they were terrified, especially His Majesty, because the princess's forty-eight hours of life were passing swiftly. She lay there now, scarcely breathing at all.

The king did not know what to do. He walked about talking to himself. *"Hélas! Que faut-il faire* (What must we do)? Now I do not care who it is, even if a wretched beggar should slay this beast, I would keep my word to him and let him marry *la princesse* if only she can be saved!"

Now, being a very religious man, the king sent for the priest to give the princess the last rites.

When the priest came, he began to pray and so did all the court, inside and outside of the palace. They knelt everywhere with lighted candles in their hands, asking God to receive this princess' soul should she die.

The sun sadly disappeared under the clouds, leaving a thick mist over all the land. Even the trees shed their leaves sorrowfully upon the ground. The birds stopped singing and they could be seen perched on the trees around the palace with big tears rolling out of their eyes. Even the little animals came from the woods and mourned for Princess Zézette.

But Zézette lay there motionless.

Now, there was a boy who used to come by the king's kitchen door to beg for scraps of brown rice cake and crumbs of cassava made with grated coconut. He used to love to sit by the fire or near the warm cinders when the mountain air was cool. Everyone started to call him Cendrillon, which means Cinderboy. Cendrillon used to tell tales and do tricks and when the king heard of him, he asked that he perform as an entertainer for the princess.

The king had grown to like him very much and had done so many things for Cendrillon that the other court servants became jealous of him. The lies that they told the king about him were unthinkable, but the king and the princess refused to believe such malicious tales.

Haitian Country Scene
(detail)

35

Well, while Princess Zézette lay close to death, one of the men who did not like Cendrillon thought this would be a good chance to get rid of him. He told the king that Cendrillon had boasted that he knew just how to handle that beast to get the ring out of his belly, if he chose to do so.

"Is that so!" exclaimed the king.

So he sent for Cendrillon.

When he arrived, the king said, "*Garçon*, did you say that you could kill that beast and restore my daughter's ring if you chose to?"

"*Non, Votre Majesté*, I did not say that I could do that."

"Whether you said it or not, you go and do it anyway. And you had better get started right now, before it is too late. If you do kill the beast, you shall marry my daughter; but if you don't kill the beast, you forfeit your head. Here is my sword. Take it and be on your way."

Poor Cendrillon was beside himself with fear. He tried to explain to the king he hadn't said that, but His Majesty would not listen.

Cendrillon did not know what to do. How was he, a timid weak boy, to slay that horrible beast which had swallowed all the best men of the island? But, since he had no choice, he took the sword and went to the forest.

At the moment when Cendrillon arrived in the forest, the beast was outside of his cave, baking in the sun.

When he saw the boy, he made ready to swallow him up.

But Cendrillon planted his feet in the ground solidly, ready to challenge the fierce beast.

The creature snapped at him again and again with his great jaws, but missed the lad each time. Cendrillon brandished the sword right and left, up and down; and finally struck the beast on the head.

Lo! the creature became so furious that smoke and fire came out his nostrils! He drove poor Cendrillon against the rock, where he couldn't move backwards or forwards. The beast opened his great jaws and prepared to swallow Cendrillon. But the boy raised his sword high and sliced the beast's jaws in two, right down to his throat.

The stricken animal roared wildly. Then he jumped in the air and when he struck the ground, the land was shaken for miles around.

Then, dying, he coughed up the ring.

Cendrillon seized the ring. He rushed to the king's palace and into Princess Zézette's chamber to find her only *just* alive.

Quickly he placed the ring on her finger; and at once she opened her eyes, smiled, and spoke. She was entirely cured.

When that happened, you can imagine how happy everybody was.

Outside the sun shone brightly. The birds fluttered their wings in the breeze and merrily they warbled together. The four-legged animals rubbed their heads together joyfully and the leaves of the trees all became lively and green under the smiling sky.

The king said to Cendrillon, "You are the bravest man in all the Caribbean Islands. You have saved my daughter's life. She shall be your bride whenever you like. Also, *mon cher prince*, whatever is in my mahogany strongbox is yours."

"There is nothing I want so much as to marry Princess Zézette," said Cendrillon.

So, at the king's request the court tailor came and made new clothes for Prince Cendrillon to wear.

Now that he was all dressed up, he looked like a born prince. In fact he was as handsome as Princess Zézette was beautiful.

All preparations were made for a great wedding. Everybody on the island attended.

Princess Zézette never again parted with her ring and she and Prince Cendrillon lived to tell their story to their grandchildren.

Harmonie Champêtre (Country Harmony)

JEAN ET MÉLISE LA CHANTEUSE
(JEAN AND MÉLISE THE SINGER)

Cric? Crac! There was once a poor man named Tonton Néré who possessed only a tiny piece of land so poor that it could grow neither congo peas nor cassava bushes. This poor man had an only son whom he called Jean. Jean had the loveliest singing voice ever heard, but his father did not appreciate it. The lad could sing the highest musical notes and the lowest as well. When he was in the mood for singing, his songs shook the trees and cracked open the ground. One day he sang so hard that he raised his little hut, with his father in it, up into the air! Tonton Néré was quite angry with him for that.

Now there was a *nganga* (witch doctor) who lived in a distant place, who had a daughter called Mélise who had begun to talk the very first day she was born. But the girl talked too much! Awake or asleep, she spoke of everything she saw. The *nganga* didn't like this. He feared that his daughter might tell what he put in the boiling cauldron to make his magic.

He scolded Mélise so severely for babbling that the girl took a vow never to talk again. She went to the top of a mountain and refused to come down. She took singing lessons from a magic bird that lived in the mountains and for years and years she stayed there, night and day, awake or asleep, in rain or in sunshine, singing away.

Presently the news spread through all the islands that Mélise, la Chanteuse, had reached the age to be wooed, but because she sang so much, she had no time to entertain young men. It was announced that her father, the *nganga*, wished that some great man singer would come and sing her into silence. As a reward he offered ten bags of money, weighing a thousand pounds each, and the singing girl as a bride. But any contestant who could not make the girl stop singing was to be put into the magic oven.

Heaven only knows how many men were put into the magic oven after that!

One day, Jean told Tonton Néré, his father, that he thought that his singing could match that of any singing girl.

"No," said Tonton Néré, "you cannot sing that well and you don't have a chance. And furthermore, you are all I have. I wouldn't live much longer if you were to go and never return. No one has been to the *nganga's* as yet and come back, dead or alive."

"But, papa," said Jean, "I'd like to try my voice there. We have lived in great poverty so long; sometimes we have nothing in our stomachs for days. Now, here is a chance to get ten bags of money and a bride besides."

So, finally, his father consented. He got up one morning and packed a little bundle for Jean. He put a few pieces of stale cassava bread in it, and a few sticks of sugarcane for him to munch on, and bade him farewell.

Tears ran down his cheeks and into his gray whiskers as he watched the boy walking away. "Farewell to you, my lad," he said.

Jean went on his journey. He waved his hand and soon was lost from sight.

Jean walked through the green mountains and valleys. Like a bird, he slept in a tree whenever night came. Finally, after several days, he came to a great lake. An island with a very high mountain stood in the middle of it.

Since it was cool there, Jean sat under a mango tree to rest awhile. He was munching on a piece of cassava bread when he saw a straw hut with smoke coming out of it on the other side of the lake. It was moving on the water like a boat and soon came to the shore where Jean was.

A woman with the longest nose he had ever seen anywhere stood in the entrance of the hut.

"God keep His sun shining on you," she said.

"The same to you," the lad replied.

"My name is Tantine Charonne. This is my hut. I use it to carry people across to the *hounfort* (magic altar) of the *nganga*."

At the mention of the *nganga*, Jean jumped to his feet. "That's where I want to go," he said.

"Then I'm sorry for you, for you haven't a chance. No more than a hundred others who have gone across in my hut have never come back, dead or alive." And she shook her long nose to sneeze, and said, "Get in, lad, if you want to cross. But first pay me with a piece of cassava bread, for I have to eat it with my fish. If you don't pay me, you'll lose your chance to end up in the *nganga*'s magic pot."

Jean gave Tantine Charonne a piece of cassava bread and went into the hut.

Tantine Charonne took the cassava bread, then stirred the water, and the hut moved toward the island. She dipped her long nose in the lake; and each time she pulled it out, half a dozen fish or more were hanging on it. That was the way she caught her fish.

She quickly landed Jean on the shore of the island.

When Jean set foot on land, a little black mule came galloping down the mountain toward him. He neighed three times, stopped and said, "Get on my back."

"And who are you?" inquired Jean.

"I'm in the service of the *nganga*," answered the black mule. "I'll take you to his place in no time."

And so, Jean got on the bare back of the mule. Before you could count to one, they were before the gate of the *nganga*.

"Oh! Oh!" cried the *nganga*, when he saw Jean coming. "Light the fire under my *chaudière* (iron kettle), and sharpen my knives well, for I see another victim coming!"

He sat there on an upturned wooden mortar, stamping his foot on the ground. Zoom! Zoom! Everything went like lightning. In a flash the fire was blazing under the cauldron and the sound of knives on grindstone filled the air.

So many men had failed to out sing Mélise, that the *nganga* was sure that no man could now stop the girl. So he prepared to put Jean in the oven. On the other hand, he had the ten bags of money brought out and a donkey to carry them, just in case the lad was able to make the girl come down from the mountaintop.

When Jean arrived, *la petite chanteuse* (the young singer) was still on the mountaintop, singing away. Jean stood and listened to her. She sang and sang like a nightingale.

"It's a good strong voice she has," Jean remarked to himself, "but I'll try to out sing her just the same."

He looked at beautiful Mélise as he stood at the foot of the mountain and he saw

Chanson pour une Demi-déesse Blessèe (Song for a Wounded semi-goddess) (detail)

Opposite page:
Humilité

and heard nothing else; not the *nganga*—nor the knives being sharpened—nor red hot fire under the cauldron which was to cook him by magic.

He began to sing. He sang and sang, and his singing was different from any the *nganga* and his people had ever heard before. First, he sang and shook the mountain so hard that he shook Mélise out of her place on the top of it.

She started down from the mountaintop.

"My goodness," cried the *nganga* stamping his foot on the ground. "He makes her come down from the mountaintop..."

But the others said, "He's got to do more than that!"

La petite chanteuse stood right before Jean and sang until she turned him into an ox. *Mon Dieu*!—that was a thing to see!

But Jean was a powerful boy. He sang so hard that he came back to himself; he sang as if thunder roared. His voice lifted Mélise up in the air and brought her down again.

They had been singing for hours. And the *nganga* warmed to Jean and smote the ground again and again and shouted, "You'll soon win her! You'll soon win her, lad! No man has been able to get her down from that mountain and sing that long. *Continuez, mon ami*," he shouted.

So Jean sang harder and harder, but the girl sang a variety of notes which took Jean's head off his body and placed it on backward. But this, instead of stopping him, made him angry. So he closed his eyes and threw his head back and sang so loudly that the ground cracked open and swallowed the girl up to her waist. Then he sang his head back where it belonged.

Everyone listened and watched in great excitement. Jean kept up the singing. "Ah!" Mélise finally gasped for breath. It was the first time in years she had said a word that was not a musical note. When that happened, the *nganga* cried,

"Aha! *Voilà*! (You see!)"

But Jean sang on.

"Ah! you. Let me out of the ground!" Mélise moaned.

But it was no use, for Jean kept on singing and the ground kept on swallowing her. "Let me out, I'll stop singing. If you let me out, I'll talk!" she cried.

But Jean didn't seem to hear her. For a moment it looked as if the ground was about to swallow her altogether. Even her chin had sunk beneath the red earth.

Finally Jean let her get out of the ground.

Her promise to stop apparently meant nothing, for she still sang. But her voice was growing weak.

The *nganga* cried and all his followers clapped their hands saying, "She soon will stop singing for good! Keep it up, my friend! Keep it up!"

Mélise was exhausted. She said, "*Laissez moi*! (Leave me alone!)" And she dropped in a heap on the ground, as though she were dead!

The *nganga* stood up and shouted, "She is through!"

But Jean kept on singing. The *nganga* thought for a moment and then said worriedly, "I wonder if he is going to keep it up, too, as she did all those years?" He groaned in despair.

And then Jean stopped.

The *nganga* took the lad's hand and said, "*Petit garçon,* you've done well with her. See, she has not yet revived." Then he pointed to the money on the ground and said, "There are your ten bags of money. When she comes to, you may put her on the donkey and take her and the money away with you. The peace and quiet I'll have is worth this much and more."

Then the *nganga* released all the men who had come before Jean, for he had not really killed them. He had only held them captive, and had promised to release them when a singing hero satisfied his desire.

Now he gave a feast, with tubs and tubs of yams, breadfruit, and green plantains cooked with goat meat and congo peas, and dozens of calabashes of *tafia* for all. The voodoo drums sounded and they all sang joyously in honor of Jean and Mélise.

When the dance was over, Mélise, *la petite chanteuse,* woke up. Jean put his reward money on the donkey's back and his bride on top of the money.

He took her home to Tonton Néré, where they were all very happy, and Jean and his bride lived to sing many years together in wealth and peace.

Deux Bonnes Femmes (Two Good Women)

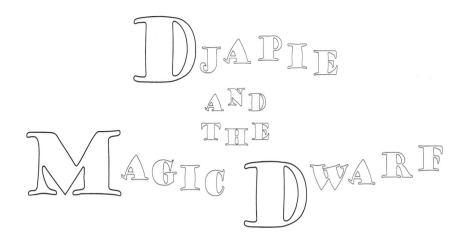

Djapie and the Magic Dwarf

Cric? Crac! Somewhere in West Africa there lived the oldest and the wisest witch doctor. He could turn people into stone and stop the roaring of the sea. He could make the moon laugh and the sun weep. He could make fire keep alight on water. He was a *housicanzo* and therefore could walk on fire without being burned.

In the same village lived a lad named Djapie, who was big and strong, strong enough to face a wild cat without fear; Djapie was a hunter.

He was not interested in anything but hunting, until one day he watched the witch doctor turn a young gazelle into a maiden.

Djapie had been so impressed that he yearned to study witchcraft himself and to become as wise and skilled as the old man. He went to him and begged that he might become his pupil.

The witch doctor, a man of wisdom, frowned. Squatting in front of his magic cauldron, he lifted his thick black brows and said, "It is well, but I know you, Djapie. You are young and careless." And this Djapie could not deny, for it was true.

"And worse than that, you are greedy and impatient. One cannot practice my art unless one is without these failings."

Djapie hung his head, but he murmured that he would try to overcome his weaknesses and to obey the witch doctor in all things.

But the being of a child and of a lad and of a man are not swiftly changed. Although Djapie studied well and learned cleverly, again and again his greed defeated him and his careless ways tripped him up and turned all his knowledge to nothing. At the end of a year's time, what he had learned amounted to scarcely more than a bag of tricks.

About this time, the strangers came to the village, made sweet promises to the people, and lured many onto a great ship.

Djapie was tempted by the wonders that they told of.

"No," said the witch doctor. "Do not listen to them, for they will take you to a far land where you will live in misery and the wonders that they speak of will be not for you, but for others."

Then he said further that these men would get those they could by cunning and wile, but those who would not come, they would take by force.

He taught a charm to Djapie that would make him resist with ease both the cleverness and the strength of these men. But when it came about as the wise man had said, and the folk of the village were thrown by force into the hold of the ship, Djapie slipped and stumbled in the charm which he had learned.

When the sails of the ship arose in the evening breeze, Djapie, too, was aboard. His little drum that hung around his neck by a string of tiger-skin was all he had to remind him of his home.

The hours passed and it grew dark. The ship tossed right and left and jumped each wave that it met.

Djapie was heavy-hearted. It was now too late; he was too far out on the ocean to go back to West Africa. If he only knew some magic charm that was strong enough to give him wings, so he could fly back home, or so he could turn the sea into solid earth and walk back home on it. His tears fell in the ocean all through the night and they seemed to have magic in them, for he saw the glorious sun climbing above the silvery horizon.

Imploringly he said, "O Sun! O Sun! Please shine on my native Africa and tell the wisest witch doctor to send a magic charm that will take me back home."

Like his tears, his words seemed to have had magic in them, for the sun spoke back to him.

"Ha-ha-ha-ha!" the sun laughed and then said, "Too late! Too late!" and it hid under a heavy gray cloud.

Mysteriously Djapie's tears turned red as they fell into the ocean. As the ship sailed on, the current carried the stream of red tears back to the land.

That day the sky was very bright and the sea was clear. As Djapie looked into the water, he saw a school of fish.

"O Fish! O Fish! Please swim back to the coast of my native Africa and tell the wisest witch doctor to send a magic charm that will take me back home."

The fish came to the surface of the water and stood on their fins.

"Ha-ha-ha-ha-ha!" they laughed and then said in a chorus, "Too late! Too late!"

And they swam under the lonely waves.

After several months of rough sailing, the ship anchored in the harbor of one of the West Indian Islands. Its mountains rose high against the blue Caribbean Sea. The island was Haiti, the Pearl of the Antilles.

The Africans were taken off the ship to the marketplace, to be sold to plantation owners.

Because Djapie was young and big and strong, he was sold quickly.

But Djapie proved to be a poor worker, so no planter kept him very long. He was sold and resold to plantation owners in every corner of the island.

This went on for several years until one day the independence of Haiti was proclaimed and all the slaves became free men.

Djapie found himself at liberty, but he still had no interest in working. Above everything, he preferred to hunt, and there were no wild animals in the Haitian jungle. So he decided to go from south to north, and from east to west, to show people those simple magic tricks he had learned, so as to be able to get food to eat.

And he did. But soon all the tricks became as stale as the witch doctor had warned him they would.

Dans une Plage Caraïbe (On the Carribean Seashore)

Again he traveled the same places; but this time he went to beg.

As soon as people found that he didn't want to work, they refused to feed him and clothe him.

One morning before dawn he arose and, crestfallen, went to the Cote-de-Fer, the Iron Cliff, where the ocean beats the rocks day and night. As he sat, weeping, Djapie felt the morning breeze blowing. He looked at the leaves of the trees.

Chanson pour une Demi-déesse Blessèe (Song for a Wounded semi-goddess) (detail)

Sadly he said, "O Breeze! O Breeze! Blow back to my native Africa and tell the wisest witch doctor to send a magic charm that will take me home."

"Ha-ha-ha-ha-ha!" the breeze laughed, and shook the leaves of the trees and said, "Too late! Too late!" and the leaves were still again.

Poor Djapie wept into the ocean; his magic tears angered the waves. They rolled like giant red carpets, which seemed to groan silently under their own weight until they struck against the rocks. Each echo resounded in the mountains beyond.

"O Waves! O Waves!" Djapie said pleadingly, "Please, strike harder. Echo back to my native Africa and tell the wisest witch doctor to send a magic charm that will take me back home."

The waves groaned louder and laughed together in a mixed chorus, "Ha-ha-ha-ha-ha!"

Then they struck the rocks harder and said, "Too late! Too late!" and became calm again.

After Djapie had wept a long time, he heard a noise coming from the horizon. He raised his head and saw something like a white foam speeding to shore. Sometimes it turned gray and sometimes it turned black and blue and then red. When it came near to the shore, Djapie saw that it was the witch doctor riding on the back of a porpoise, a sword-fish on each side of him.

"O Master! O Master!" Djapie cried. "Please use your magic to take me back to my native Africa. I still want to become a witch doctor as wise as you."

The witch doctor replied, "Too late now! Too late now! I only came to ask you why you don't use the magic I've taught you!"

"I've used all the tricks. They became too stale for use."

"Well," said the witch doctor, "here is a seashell. With it you can do many things, if you can remember how I once taught you to prepare it. But be sure you stop using it when ninety days and ninety nights have passed, or you'll have bad luck."

He reached out until he could touch Djapie's outstretched hands and placed in them a small coiled shell that was rough to the touch. Then he went away on the back of the porpoise, cutting through the waves, before Djapie could speak again.

Djapie had such strong faith in the magic of the shell that, for the first time in his life, he forgot that he didn't like to work. He constructed a forge and built a fire on it, then took a pinch of white tufa, a handful of *metsignin* leaves and threw them in. Next he sprinkled three handfuls of salt water from the ocean on them, to make magic-iron.

And soon he had enough magic-iron to start to work.

For ten days and nights, the red fire in the forge never went out and the echo of the strokes made by Djapie's hammer on the anvil never ceased resounding in the mountains. On the tenth day, after having smoothed out the iron several times, he had made a large three-legged iron cauldron and a long spoon with three little fiery-eyed owls standing on the tip of its handle. He then ordered the spoon and the three-legged pot to go and get some water.

The spoon hopped ahead obediently, and the three-legged pot followed clumsily, swaying from right to left.

When they were at a distance from the forge, the spoon took one dewdrop and put it into the pot. They both walked back to the master's den.

Now Djapie kindled a fire with seven handfuls of wild fig leaves. He lit it by sprinkling a little water over it. The fire came up and the dewdrop began to fill the pot. Djapie picked seven little leaves from seven different weeds and put them in the pot. Then he added a few sweet weeds and some acid weeds, some sweet twigs and some acid twigs.

The pot began to boil. Djapie stirred it with the long spoon. It sent up red, black, blue, green, and snow white fumes, which are the signs of good magic.

Then Djapie dropped the seashell into it.

Now he beat his little drum that hung from its tiger-skin string. He took quick leaps around the magic cauldron, making a little squeaky noise at each leap. The spoon leaped behind him. The leaves of a huge mapou-tree that sheltered him stood on end. The three little owls on the tip of the spoon handle came to life.

"Hou! Hou! Hou!" they cried as they flew in circles over Djapie's head.

Then Djapie stood with his hands spread out over the cauldron, moving them up as if to draw something out of it. Each time he did that, the water in the magic pot tried to follow his hands upward, but splashed back again, making a sound like the roaring of thunder. After the pot had sizzled for a few hours, the three owls dove into it one after another.

Then came a loud "Whizz!" followed by an explosion.

Boom! Lo!

A magic dwarf, dressed in a ceremonial costume, jumped out of the pot, a little flute in his hand. The three owls flew out behind him and then perched on the boughs of the mapou-tree.

The dwarf began to play his flute and dance, while Djapie beat his drum. Now he began to direct the dwarf.

"Jump right, jump left; swing right, swing left. Throw your head back and turn on your heels."

And, as the dwarf danced and he played his flute, an idea came to Djapie.

He decided to go from town to town and make the dwarf play his flute and dance while he, Djapie, would beat the drum to accompany him. In that way, he could collect much money.

So, with the dwarf on his shoulder and the owls flying after him, Djapie went from place to place, acclaimed by all.

After he had performed in many towns and collected much money, the three owls, one after the other, said, "Hou! Hou! Hou! Ninety days and ninety nights have nearly come to pass!"

Djapie paid no attention to them.

When the owls continued to say "Ninety days and ninety nights have nearly come to pass," Djapie was annoyed and said, "My ninety days and ninety nights have not yet come to pass. I'm the one to know when that comes."

So he went on, hoping to fill his hat, which was not yet quite full of coins. When he arrived at a place called *Quanaminth*, he found the people waiting impatiently to see him and his dwarf perform together.

But the owls flew overhead, hooting together, "Hou! Hou! Hou! Ninety days and ninety nights have come to pass!"

Djapie paid no attention to the warning of the owls. He stood in the public square and ordered the dwarf to perform as before, but the dwarf did not budge.

He was like a lifeless wooden doll.

The people laughed at Djapie scornfully.

He became so angry and impatient with the lifeless dwarf that he pulled the flute away from him and broke it into two pieces. And, lo! the dwarf jumped in the air and, when he hit the ground, he turned into the same seashell that the witch doctor had given Djapie.

And all the money in his pockets disappeared.

Carnaval Haitien (Haitian Carnival) (detail)

Paysage Haitien (Haitian Scene)

The audience shuddered.

Djapie picked up the shell and walked away from the silent crowd, the three owls still flying after him.

He thought it might be worth his while to boil the shell in the magic cauldron once again.

Away from the people, Djapie stopped to see what magic power he had left. He called the pot and asked it to come to him from where he had left it in the south, but the pot did not come.

Djapie's magic was gone, so he had to walk to the south of the island.

It took him many days, but at last one early morning he arrived and found the pot and the spoon where he had left them by the mapou-tree. He himself put one drop of the water in the pot, because the pot and the spoon refused to do it. Then Djapie put some green leaves under the pot and tried to light them with a sprinkle of water as he did before. But the fire would not catch. So Djapie was forced to use a few dried twigs and a little dried kindling wood and light them in the usual way.

The flame rose under the magic cauldron, but the dewdrop failed to fill up the pot, so Djapie had to fetch a couple of calabashes of spring water from many miles away to fill it. He put all the ingredients into it and stirred constantly with his long spoon.

It showed no vari-colored fumes as it did the first time. When it boiled Djapie dropped the seashell into it, but the shell jumped right out and hit the ground. There was no magic noise, no explosion, and no dwarf came out.

Djapie cooked the shell and stirred it for a whole day and part of the night, but nothing happened.

He placed the shell on the ground in front of him, took a heavy mallet and raised it in the air as high as his arms could go, so as to smash the shell into a thousand pieces. But before he knew what was happening, the shell disappeared and the magic hammer struck the earth. The ground cracked and opened and swallowed Djapie up.

In the rays of the moonlight, the three owls hovered and looked down upon the spot where Djapie had disappeared. They hooted in succession,

"Hou?"

"Hou?"

"Hou?"

Then they perched on the bough of the mapou-tree, looking at one another as they remarked in turn,

"His greed had no ears."

"His greed for more increased with each silver coin."

"His greed killed his good sense and then pushed him to excess and then to his doom."

At that, the three owls disappeared in the air.

Voodoo Priestess

THE COCKROACH AND THE HEN

There was once a country cockroach who gave her little baby to a city hen as a godchild.

When the little roach grew big enough to go to school, the Hen asked the Cockroach to send him to her so she could teach him religion and have him educated. Those things, the Hen said, were her duties as a godmother.

Cockroach knew that the Hen was very rich, as she lived in a big cement house and she associated only with the elite. Little Roach would have many advantages and would learn good manners at the godmother's expense. Cockroach was delighted with the idea. She packed Little Roach's things and took him to his godmother.

For a long time, Little Roach got along very well with his godmother. But one day when she was caressing him with her beak, accidently one of Little Roach's legs broke off. Hen ate the leg. It was so delicious that she lost her head and ate Little Roach up entirely.

When Hen came to her senses and realized what she had done, she was panicky. "I've done the worst thing in my life," she said, flapping her wings up and down, and down and up. "I've eaten my godchild. What shall I tell Cockroach when she comes to see Little Roach?"

A few days later, Cockroach came to see her child, bringing a *calabash* of cane syrup and some cassava bread for him. "Good day to you, Hen," she said. "How is Little Roach getting along? I want to see him, to caress him a little. You will agree, Hen, that there is nothing so important to a child as his mother's love."

With forced gaiety, the Hen smiled and said, "Isn't it too bad, you've just missed Little Roach. I sent him to buy some syrup in the marketplace. He won't be back until evening."

Cockroach bade Hen good day and left.

But when Cockroach came back the next day, Hen told her that Little Roach had gone fishing with some friends long before daylight and would not be back until night.

This happened several times until Cockroach became worried. She went to several of her lady cockroach friends, and told them of the constant absence of Little Roach.

"Ah, Cockroach," said one of them, "I wouldn't trust Hen. In fact the neighbors thought you had lost your wits when you sent the child to her. She is not to be trusted. For all you know Hen might be a follower of voodooism."

"Heaven only knows what might have happened to Little Roach, for we haven't seen him playing on the porch for a long time," said another cockroach.

"If I were you, Cousin Cockroach," said a distant relative, "I would check up on Hen."

All this almost drove Cockroach crazy. She ran back to town to Hen's house. When she got there, Little Roach was not there. Hen said that he was still out fishing with friends.

Cockroach became angry and demanded her child. Finally Hen broke down and confessed. But she swore, crossing her beak on the ground twice in the form of a cross, that she had nothing to do with the disappearance of Little Roach, but an old *diablesse* (she-devil) had seized him and carried him off.

"Which way did she take him?" asked the mother. "I'll go after her and get my child back."

"It's too late, Cockroach," said the Hen, "for the old witch ate him in mid-air. That's why I've been grieving so much."

60

The Cockroach wept and wept.

The Hen joined her in weeping and promised to avenge her godchild.

Sadly the Cockroach went home to the mountains.

Hen thought that Cockroach might be suspicious of the dirty deed. She went to a *papa houngan* (witch doctor) to get a voodoo charm in order to protect herself, just in case Cockroach sent a *zombi* after her. She told her story to the voodoo doctor who said, "The solution is simple."

"What do you mean, papa?" asked the Hen.

"You have only to eat all the cockroaches on the island the same way you ate Little Roach," he advised.

"How can I ever eat all the cockroaches on the island?" Hen asked.

"First of all," said the voodoo doctor, "get all the cockroaches in one room together and do it this way:

"Go and tell Cockroach that you have a way to avenge your godchild. Tell her that you are inviting the *diablesse* to a party given especially for her, and she, Cockroach, must come and bring all the cockroaches in Haiti to the party. Tell her that when the *diablesse* comes that she and her friends must fall on her and help you kill her. This is just a make-believe, you see," the *houngan* said. "Tell her also that there will be many chickens at the party, so she will not be disturbed upon seeing so many. Moreover, make it clear to Cockroach that the voodoo drums will echo in the mountains so all the cockroaches in the land will be interested and attend.

"But," he went on, "invite all the chickens in the land to come to the party, too, so they can help you eat the cockroaches and this is no make-believe!" the *houngan* said with mocking smile. "Also, you must hire a mouse orchestra from the mountains to play some voodoo rhythm. You know, the cockroaches are country folks, and there is nothing they like better than to dance a good round of voodoo dance. And don't forget to hire a dog, a monkey, and a cat to be the doorkeepers."

Now the *houngan* gave Hen a phial of voodoo compound. She was to put it in a punch and serve it to the cockroaches. After they drank it and became intoxicated, she was to give the signal to the doorkeepers who would shut the doors. The chickens would do the rest.

Hen went directly to Cockroach's house who was very happy to hear of the plan to avenge her child.

Then, as the *houngan* had directed, Hen also went to every chicken's house. She invited the roosters and the young chickens all to come and help her eat cockroaches. She suggested that they should not eat anything for twenty-four hours so that they would be good and hungry.

When the hour for the party arrived, hen's house was beautifully decorated. The punch was on the table, ready for the guests. The orchestra of mice, with their voodoo drums, tambourines, and gourd rattles were sitting on the porch ready to play. The monkey, the dog, and the cat doorkeepers were at their posts.

Carnaval Haitien (Haitian Carnival) (detail)

Cockroaches and chickens from all over Haiti came to the party, for they loved parties flavored with voodooism. They talked and laughed and drank. The orchestra played a vigorous rhythmic voodoo tune. Chickens and cockroaches began to dance. They danced and the roaches drank, but the chickens only pretended to drink. Soon all the cockroaches lost their heads. They were not at all conscious that they were showing the city folks the real way they danced the voodoo under the spell of the voodoo potion.

One who was possessed by the voodoo god *Papa Guédé*, wore a black suit, a torn and tattered hat, and smoked a huge cigar. They all closed their eyes and savagely danced the African dances.

When Hen saw that they were fully intoxicated, she gave the signal to the doorkeepers. In the twinkling of an eye, the windows and the doors were shut tight and heavy logs were put behind them.

The chickens fell upon the intoxicated cockroaches and ate every one of them, legs, wings, heads, and all.

But there was one little cockroach who was not affected by the voodoo potion. He remained alive and escaped unseen as soon as the doors were reopened.

And he is the ancestor of all the cockroaches in Haiti today. The Haitian chickens still chase and eat cockroaches, but they will never be rid of them all, as some will always find a way to escape.

Félicité
(detail)

Cric? Crac! The following original folktales, from the 1949 published volume of *Children of Yayoute,* are told in a traditional Haitian way. Developed from African stories handed down for generations, you will meet Malice, the trickster, and Bouqui, the gullible. In the tales we have selected, you will see that fate has a few tricks in store for Malice and a triumph or two for Bouqui.

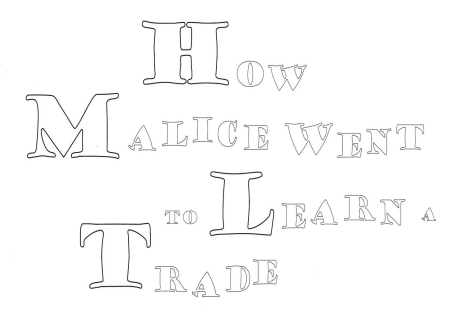

How Malice Went to Learn a Trade

Compère Macaque, the monkey, Commère Macaque, his wife, and Ti-Macaque, their young one, carrying their long tails on their arms, were passing before Malice's house when Compère Macaque stopped and said,

"Look at Compère Malice, still lying on his back in the same spot where we saw him when we passed by this morning."

"I hope you won't be as lazy as your godfather Malice, Ti-Macaque, when you grow up," said Commère Macaque. Turning to Compère Macaque she said, "If it were left to me, Malice wouldn't be the godfather of my child; it was all your idea."

"Compère Malice is all right, if you understand him. Hola, Compère Malice," Compère Macaque cried.

"Hola, godfather Malice," Ti-Macaque cried.

"Hola, Commère, Compère, and Ti-Macaque! And your health?"

"Not bad, Compère Malice!" replied the three in turn.

"Won't you come in and have a cup of coffee? I have a new bag of coffee which makes delicious coffee, yes."

"No, thank you, Compère Malice. We want to get home before it gets completely dark."

They turned around the curve.

"Have you ever heard why Compère Malice is so lazy and tricky?" Commère Macaque asked. "They say that he learned it from a teacher, a real teacher."

"Don't tell me. No! That could not be true," Compère Macaque said with a laugh.

"That's true. I was told that it was in the days when Malice was young. Mère Malice could never get him to do any work. He would not even go into the kitchen to get his food if he could find someone to bring it to him.

"One day they say that Mère Malice called him, 'Malice, get up from your back and dig some yams for supper.'

" 'I can't do it, maman, because I'd have to bend my back to dig it, and that's too much work for me to do.'

" 'As the old saying goes,' said Mère Malice, 'Maman donkey bears her colt to help her carry the load on her back, but as for you, Malice, it seems that I bore you to add to my burden.'

She went into the field and dug the yams herself. But a few minutes later she called, 'Malice, child, go get some kindling wood to start the fire under the pot.'

Paysage Haitien (Haitian Scene) (detail)

66

Harmonie Champêtre (Country Harmony) (detail)

" 'I can't do it. It's too far for me to walk; my legs might get tired.'

"She had to go after the wood and then build the fire herself. But a while later she called, 'Malice, get up from your back and bring me the gourds so I can dish up the food so we can eat.'

" 'I'm sorry, maman. I'm too tired to do that.'

" 'How can you be tired when you have been lying on your back since daylight, and now the sun is behind Mount La Selle?'

"She went after the gourds and dished the food into them. 'Malice, your food is ready. The only thing you have to do now is come and get it and eat.'

"Malice still lay on his back with his legs crossed, his hands under his head, and his hat over his face. 'Please, maman, bring it to me. The gourd may be too heavy for me to lift,' he said.

67

" 'If it's too heavy, it means there's too much food in it. I'll take some out so you can lift it.'

" 'No, maman,' Malice said as he jumped up. 'I'll try to get it. Don't take any of it out.'

"He walked as slowly as if he were going to a wedding, as we say. Finally he arrived in the kitchen and took his gourd of dried goat meat stew with potatoes and yams and congo peas. Then he sat down and began to eat.

"Mère Malice sat down, too, and began to eat her portion of the stew. After a minute or so, she said, 'Malice, you lie on your back so much, I should think you would get a sore on it. And as lazy as you are, I don't know what you're going to be when you grow up. You won't work; you won't go to chapel or school.'

" 'I don't see why I should waste my time going to school. It's too much trouble for me to open a book and read it. The others are so mean that they won't open it and tell me what's in it. Besides that, I would have to carry the books. When I get there I would have to sit up too long. That would tire me out.'

"Poor Mère Malice had tried every way she could to get Malice interested in some sort of work. Now after thinking a second, she said, 'In the morning I want you to go to the village and speak to one of the trademasters there. Maybe a hat maker or a shoemaker, so he can teach you his trade. I don't want to hear that you aren't going. You'll go if I have to chase you with a firebrand.'

" 'You won't have to do that, maman. I'll be glad to go.'

" 'At last!' she said, happily seeing that for once Malice was interested in work.

" 'I'll go the first thing in the morning, but I'll have to find one who won't ask me to do anything hard or lift anything heavy.'

"The next morning Malice got up and went to the foot of the village where all the trademasters' shops were. He went into a shop, but came out saying to himself, 'Not a blacksmith! I couldn't lift one of those horse shoes.' So he went into another place where the master taught hat weaving. But Malice came right out again saying to himself, 'Not me! No indeed! My fingers would be too tired weaving hats.'

"So he kept on going from place to place until finally he went into an empty shop where there were no tools. The boss, a very fat fellow, lay on his back with his eyes closed.

" 'This looks more like the place where I belong,' Malice said to himself. He walked up to the man and said, 'Boss, I would like to know what trade you teach. I want to learn it.'

"The man said nothing.

" 'He can't be dead because he is breathing,' Malice said. He called again, 'Boss, I want to learn your trade.'

"The man twisted himself lazily, mumbling, 'Why do you come and make me talk? That's too much trouble, too much work for a poor man.'

" 'Ah!' Malice breathed with enthusiasm. 'You'll be interested in me if you will only listen to me. I think I have talent.'

" 'What do you want?' the man asked impatiently.

" 'I've been trying to tell you that I want to learn your trade,' answered Malice.

" 'Nobody can learn my trade,' replied the man. 'I'm the only lazybones and trickster-master in the land. I can easily teach you to be lazy, but it is hard to be a good trickster.'

" 'I don't think it'll be hard because it is the only trade that interests me.'

" 'No use,' said the boss. 'It's hard enough to think of teaching you, but I'd have to be thinking and talking to you. That's too much work for me.'

" 'But you won't be sorry if you take me in,' Malice said.

" 'Alright. I'll try you out. But as I've said, it will be easy to learn to be a lazybones; but as for a trickster, if you can learn it so well that you're better than I, you can put me out of my shop and take it over. I'm sorry, you're going to waste your time and mine.'

" 'I'll take the chance, boss,' Malice said.

"So he began to take lessons right away. It didn't take him long at all to master the art of being a lazybones, as the boss had told him. But it was sometime later that the boss decided to see how much Malice had learned as a trickster. He sent him to trick people who didn't have much experience. Malice did very well every time. The boss decided to try him on people who were more on the alert.

"One day, apprentice and boss were standing at the foot of the hill when the boss said, 'I see you're learning fast, Malice.'

69

Le Triage des Grains (The Grain Harvest)

" 'Yes, thank you. It's because you've taught me well.'

"At that moment the boss saw a man with a goat going around a nearby curve. He said to Malice, 'I want you to go and trick the goat right out of that man's hand, without causing any trouble. After you've done so, take the goat back and place the rope in his hand without his knowing it.'

"Malice looked somewhat puzzled. He didn't see how he could do that. But he went just the same. When he saw the man walking as if he had bad feet, an idea came to him. He ran home, picked a pair of *zapate* (sandals), and sped across the woods ahead of the man and his goat. Then he put one of the *zapate* in the center of the road and hid behind a bush and watched.

"The poor fellow was limping along, leading his goat by a rope, when he saw the *zapate*. He looked at it, picked it up, and examined it. 'This is a good *zapate*, but what good will it be for my two sore feet?'

"He threw it alongside the road and went on his way.

"Malice came out of his hiding place and, by a shortcut, got ahead of the man again. He laid the other *zapate* in the center of the road and quickly hid behind a bush again.

"'Ai-ai-ai! My grandmother told me that I was born dumb and would die dumb. I believe her now because if I

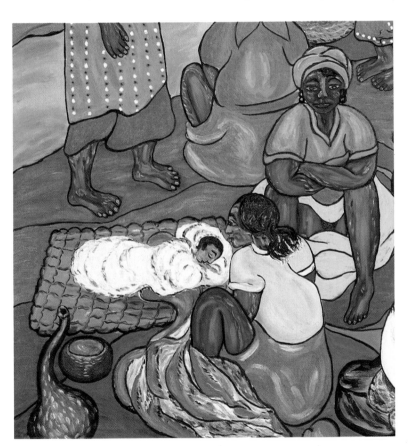

Paysage Haitien (Haitian Scene) (detail)

had sense, I would have picked up the other *zapate* and had a pair for my sore feet. I'm going after it; maybe it's still there.'

"So he tied the goat to a tree and walked back. Then Malice came out of his hiding place and took the goat to his boss. The boss was very surprised to see Malice with the goods. He couldn't imagine how he had tricked the animal away from the man without causing any trouble.

" 'It looks as if he is better than I am already. I couldn't have tricked the beast away from the man like that,' the boss said to himself. 'But I'll give him a more difficult task. I'll send him after something we won't be able to find anywhere. I've got to stop him or he'll really take my trade away from me.'

"In the meantime, Malice took the goat back and found the man who had searched for his goat until, exhausted, he fell sound asleep on the ground. It wasn't hard then for Malice to put the goat's rope back in his hand. That worried the boss still more. To him, Malice was clever beyond words.

"From then on the boss tried very hard to think of something impossible for Malice to do. One day he told him, 'You've done so well that I don't think there is anybody in the land you won't trick.'

"Malice smiled very cunningly. 'I don't think I'm so good, boss, but if you say that I am, it must be true.'

" 'It's good he doesn't know he is so good. That'll make it easier to get him out of the trade,' said the master to himself. Then he said aloud to Malice, 'This time I want you to take your straw bag and go to the countryside and trick somebody out of a bagful of ouch and bring it back to me.'

" 'You want me to bring you a bag of ouch?' Malice asked.

" 'Yes, a bag of ouch.'

" 'But ouch is nothing. It's only a sound people make when something hurts them.'

" 'I know it, but if you want to become a good trickster, you must obey my command, or you'll be no trickster at all.'

"The whole thing sounded crazy to Malice. But he began walking along the mountainside repeating, 'Ouch . . . ouch . . . Where am I going to find such a thing?'

"The thought of it gave Malice such a terrible headache that he could no longer stand on his feet. So he went into the woods to look for a soft spot to lie down. He laid his straw bag aside and began to lie down. But when he was half way down, he jumped and yelled, 'Oh, ouch!' in an agonized tone. When he looked down he saw that he was on a pile of thorny cousin-seeds. He brushed them off his trousers and giggled.

" 'Good father God is good, good father God is great. Well, by the time I get back to the shop, my headache will be gone.'

"He filled his bag with cousin-seeds and went back to the boss, who was waiting for him.

" 'I've fooled him, my impertinent apprentice, who thinks he can win my trade from me. I knew he'd never find that ouch, because there is no such thing that anybody can lay hands on. This time I'm going to get rid of him,' the boss thought as he waited for Malice to return.

"As Malice came into the shop the boss began to laugh deep down in his stomach, 'Ha-ha, my clever apprentice, have you brought the ouch?'

" 'Yes, boss, I have it right in my bag.'

"The boss was surprised. 'You're joking. You couldn't have found that!'

" 'You only have to put your hand in the bag to get it,' Malice said. 'And since ouch is so slippery, you had better get it with both hands.'

"It was through sheer curiosity that the boss plunged both his hands all the way to the bottom of the bag. Right away his face froze and he yelled, 'Ouch! Ouch!' Then he pulled his hands out of the bag. They were covered with the thorny cousin-seeds which stuck in his skin. 'Ouch,' he yelled again and again. Then he said to Malice, 'Young man, you've won. From now on I want to pay you to teach me the trade.'

" 'I'll teach you only on one condition. You must get a gourd of sand and count every grain of it, then tell me how many grains it holds.'

"But since the man couldn't do that, Malice became the first class trickster in the land," said Commère Macaque.

"God, my father, who could have made up this story about Compère Malice?" said Compère Macaque.

"Made up, did you say? It may be made up, but it sounds like the truth."

"How could it be true when no one has ever heard of any such teacher or any such shop where these trades were taught? Besides, we all know that not Mère Malice, but Grand-Mère Bouqui brought Malice up," said Compère Macaque.

"It's a made up story, then, but I'm afraid Ti-Macaque is going to be like his godfather. You know that it is the belief of everyone in the country that a child inherits the brain of those who hold the candle over his head in church," Commère Macaque said.

Carrying their tails on their arms, Compère Macaque, Commère Macaque, and Ti-Macaque disappeared into the twilight of the evening.

Présentation au Temple (Offering at the Temple)

Les Deux Commères (Two Gossipers)

75

The King's Cherished Lamb

It was impossible for the king to be without a pet animal. After he had lost his big bull and a cow, he acquired a young lamb which he cherished even more than the two former pets.

One day, Malice decided that he would like to eat a few lamb cutlets and he saw no other lamb whose chops would tickle his palate more. So he stole the king's lamb, killed it, skinned it, carefully saving the skin, and had a great feast all by himself.

In the morning, the king sent for the lamb to be brought to his bedside as he did every morning. But the man rushed back in great alarm and reported that the lamb had disappeared. The King leaped out of bed in great alarm, too, and sent for the *houngan*, the most successful sorcerer/fortune-teller in the country, to ask him what had become of his pet.

After the *houngan* had gone through the usual ceremony, he said, "Your lamb, my king, has already been killed and is totally consumed. The only thing I can tell you is that the shrewdest man in the land committed the deed. Now hear me, King, the shrewdest man in the land . . ."

The king had a good idea who the shrewdest man in the land was. So he sent his

76

guards after the thief. They were not to come back without him. If they did, their heads would be chopped off.

The frightened guards bowed, scraped the ground, and ran away in search of the thief.

Although the lamb was not found, the king arranged a wake for him that night.

That same afternoon, Malice, who was becoming more and more scared of his deed, met Bouqui and the two discussed the wake at the king's court.

"The king is giving prizes at the wake," Malice said.

"Prizes? What for?" Bouqui asked.

"He'll give a fat cow and two goats to whoever wears the prettiest suit made of lamb's skin and who can sing the loveliest hymn. It's too bad you can't sing," Malice said.

"I'll give you money to buy me a suit. We've been good friends long enough for you to do this for me. You'll teach me a hymn, too. If I win, half will be yours," Bouqui proposed.

Of course Malice was delighted to teach Bouqui a hymn. When it was time, he covered Bouqui's back with the lamb's skin and both went to the wake.

When they arrived, the wake was at its height. In the courtyard, groups of men played cards and shot dice. Others formed circles and told stories. Women came with their stools to sell bread, candies, rum, and tobacco. Coffee and *maté* were served as the king mourned.

At once Bouqui joined the group singing hymns and he sang the song which Malice taught him as a solo.

"Tis I—'tis I, Tonton Bouqui,
Who went into the king's stable,
And stole the king's lamb—
the lamb which I cooked with eggplant
Into a delicious *calalou*;
Now its skin is right on my back
With the king's name in black and white."

"Who sang that song? Come forward and sing it again," commanded the king.

Shyly Bouqui turned and looked at Malice.

"Don't stand there grinning with every tooth in your head. Go and sing for the king," Malice said in a low voice.

*Le Marché Haïtien
(Haitian Market)
(detail)*

Already Bouqui felt that he had won the prize. He walked before the king, his face beaming, and sang again.

"Turn around and let me look at your suit!" the king ordered after Bouqui finished the song.

Bouqui turned around.

"Seize him," cried the king. "He is the one who killed my lamb. He is wearing the skin with my initial stamped on it. Burn his back with a hot iron!"

Bouqui was seized and then tied to a tree, while the men waited for a long flat piece of iron to get hot. When it was very hot they untied Bouqui, who offered no resistance. The people made a circle and waited breathlessly for the red-hot iron to burn poor innocent Bouqui. The iron had come and the executioners were ready to apply it when the king's voice rose above the voices of the chattering crowd.

"Stop! Don't burn the man. I pardon him because firstly he is honest, or he wouldn't have confessed his crime. Secondly, he is brave because he was ready to

Conversation à Trois (Three Conversing)

take his punishment without any protest. For his honesty, give him a steer, a heifer, and three male and three female sheep so he can raise his own lambs."

Now Malice did not expect this to happen. He began to annoy Bouqui about giving him half of what the king gave him. The king, who heard Malice, ordered the guards to give him a good whipping with a *cocomacaque* (long stick) for molesting honest Bouqui.

Bouqui, who felt that Malice was responsible for his troubles, went away laughing as he said, "Sometimes the *cocomacaque* changes hand."

Malice went home well whipped and was lucky that the king did not find out that it was he who had stolen the lamb and tried to make Bouqui suffer the consequences.

How Malice Sent the Donkey to Marry the King

In the days when Malice was still a boy and was in the king's service, the sign of laziness was already beginning to show in him. He complained about everything he was told to do; even if he were to carry something as light as a *colibri* (hummingbird) feather. He was so lazy that his bones were always aching. One day he got the king so angry with his complaints that His Majesty gave him the punishment commonly inflicted on children by the peasants—a good whipping with guava switches, which stung his legs terribly. Malice became very angry and ran away from the king's service on the spot. But he swore that he was going to play at least one good trick for that whipping.

After Malice left him, the king took Bouqui into his service. Bouqui was as slow-witted as ever and always willing to accept commands if they were not too complicated. He would weed and water the flower garden and lift heavy things around the palace.

In spite of the fact that the king had a big palace, trunks full of gold under his bed, and everything anyone could wish for, there was one thing lacking in his life, a

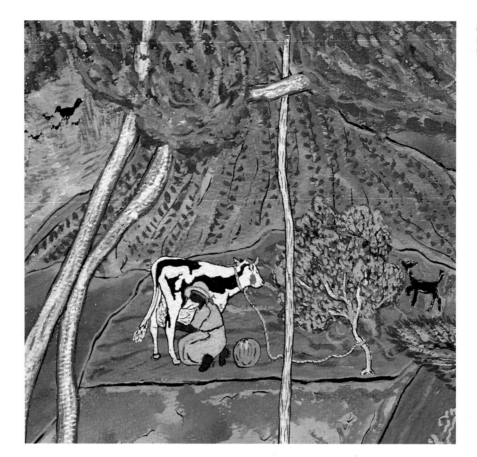

queen. He had never been married. Now he wanted a young queen and he had the girl in mind.

Since in that country people of royal lineage married whomever they wanted, whether of royal or common blood, he selected the daughter of one of his brigadiers. She was pretty and young. The king felt that he would do the brigadier a great honor by marrying his daughter and thought the girl would be so happy about the whole thing that she would willingly marry him on the spot.

So he called the brigadier and told him his wishes. He said that after he had married the girl, he would build her father a fine house, give him a couple of cows, a donkey, and a bag of gold—and maybe a knighthood later.

Upon hearing all this, the brigadier smiled broadly. He would love to have the house and animals, but there were other things involved.

Conte Vaudouesque (Voodoo Story)

"But, Your Majesty, Liza has a love affair with the boy who takes care of the pigs," said the brigadier.

"Send the boy away. Liza will be so glad to be my queen that she won't mind it at all."

"But, Your Majesty, Liza and the boy are very much in love with each other."

But the king always got what he wanted. He commanded the brigadier, "Go and make her take her mind off the pig boy. And if you know what's good for you, you'd better tell me that you'll bring her to me or you'll be put to death."

The hapless father began to worry. But after a moment he thought that since his daughter was just a child, her mind could be easily changed. She could be persuaded to marry the king who had so much gold.

"Your Majesty, I'm sure I can arrange everything with Liza as you want it. You can make all your plans for the engagement reception and send for her when everything is ready."

The brigadier went away, and the king began making preparations for the engagement reception.

But while the two were talking, Bouqui was working in the flower garden and listening to all that they said. As soon as they parted, he dropped his tools and ran to find Malice. "Malice, Compère, come and listen to what I've just heard."

Malice came over. "What?"

"Oh-oh!" Bouqui grunted. "Some people are so lucky and they don't even know it. I've just heard the king say to the brigadier that he would give a house, two cows, a donkey, and a bag of gold in exchange for Liza. The brigadier didn't want to exchange his daughter, but the king said that if he didn't, he would lose his head. So, now the king is getting things ready for the engagement reception. And just listen to this, Malice. The king said that I'm to go and bring Liza to him when everything is ready."

"What! Would you like to have a custard-apple, Bouqui?"

"Yes, I would, but I'd love to have those two cows to eat and that donkey the king wants to give to the brigadier in exchange for his daughter. But I'll take the custard-apple," Bouqui said.

"I'll give you a custard-apple if, when the king sends you after Liza, you come and tell me beforehand," Malice said.

"Make it two custard-apples."

"Good. But I'll give you one now and, after you tell me when you are going after Liza, I'll give you the other, or you might forget."

Bouqui got one big custard-apple and ate greedily.

At last the day for the engagement reception arrived. The palace was brightened up with all sorts of decorations. When all the guests were present, the king sent Bouqui for Liza.

"Bouqui, be on your way. And if you don't come back with her in the shake of a lamb's tail, I'll give you the worst whipping of your life."

Bouqui ran. He kicked up a cloud of dust which rose high behind him. He didn't want to be whipped with those guava switches. But first he ran to Malice to tell him that he was on his way to get Liza.

When Malice heard the news he grinned with every tooth in his head. "Now I'll take you to where Liza is. She is grazing on the plain."

"Grazing!" Bouqui exclaimed. "I've never known her to graze. Since when has she become a mule?"

"Come on, you'll see for yourself," Malice said.

So Bouqui trotted behind Malice across the plain. And when they arrived, Malice showed him Liza. Bouqui gulped, for the Liza he saw was not at all the one he was going after.

"Oh-oh," Bouqui grunted as he began to laugh. He laughed until he was in pain. Finally he held his stomach with both hands and said, "Malice, the king doesn't want Liza, the donkey. He wants Liza, the brigadier's daughter."

"But no," Malice assured him. "You're all wrong. He wants Liza, the donkey."

Bouqui frowned. "That's strange. Why would the king want to get engaged to a donkey?"

"But yes, he does, trust me. I used to work for the king and I know just what he wants."

So both jumped on the donkey's back to hurry to the palace. When they arrived, they jumped off and Bouqui left the donkey behind the palace and ran inside to the king.

"Has she come?"

"Yes, Your Majesty. I left her waiting outside of the back door."

"Now take her upstairs to the master room which will be hers when we are married," the king said.

"But, Your Majesty..." Bouqui said.

Présentation au Temple (Offering at the Temple) (detail)

But before he had finished his sentence the king shook his fist at him. "No buts from you. I command you. If you have to, ask some of the others back there to help you take her up."

Bouqui went out, and the king took his handkerchief and wiped the perspiration off his royal forehead. He said to one of the guests, "After all, the girl hasn't been used to the palace. She's probably a little nervous."

Bouqui ran to the back and got Malice to help him take Liza upstairs. He pulled on the rope in front and Malice pushed from the rear. After a good bit of struggle, they finally got the donkey into the big room where beautiful gowns were laid out on the bed. Six lady's maids were waiting with instructions from the king to dress the future queen and to notify the king when she was dressed.

The maids thought something was wrong that the king wanted them to dress the

Une Femme Assise (Sitting Woman)

donkey in all those beautiful fineries, but one of them said that, if they knew what was good for them, they had better dress the donkey as His Majesty had commanded.

Well, after some difficulties, they finally got her dressed. She was wearing two beautiful pairs of white satin sandals and a lovely crown was on her head.

Now one of the maids went down to tell the king that his future queen was dressed.

"Bring her down immediately," the king commanded. "And when she comes to the last step I'll take her by the arm myself."

The maid went back with the message from the king and she giggled as she told the others, "My dears, His Majesty will have to take his future queen by the foot instead of by the arm." And she laughed.

Now they started down the steps with the donkey. She made it much easier going down than going up, but just the same, you can imagine the fuss she made with her four shoes falling from her feet and held fast to her ankles only by the strings. When she came to the last step, she did not wait to be introduced or give the king the pleasure of taking her by the foot. She made her way into the parlor among the guests with her two hind feet in the air, kicking in every direction, upsetting the furniture. Some of the guests screamed, some chuckled, and some laughed loudly when the king's betrothed made her way out into the field with her crown still on her head and the train of her white gown flying high over her back.

The poor king fainted. But Malice, who was looking in from the outside, came in chuckling. He had the presence of mind to throw a tub full of cold water on the king who was still lying on his back in the middle of the reception hall. Then Malice slipped out before the king came to.

After this engagement reception you wouldn't think His Majesty would ever want to become engaged again. But he did. He married and had many children; and Malice kept on playing tricks on him.

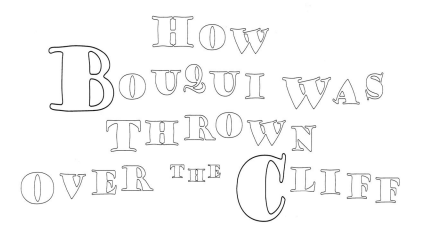

How Bouqui was Thrown over the Cliff

Bouqui went hunting wild goats and caught a tiny kid. After he had put a rope around its neck and tied its four feet, he said, "Beautiful little kid, how beautiful your throat is," caressing the kid's throat with his hand.

"That's the throat with which I sing beautiful little songs. If you wish, I'll sing to you."

"Yes, yes, sing little kid," Bouqui said.

"Baa, baa, Compère Bouqui, baa, baa.
My maman has left me behind,
My papa has left me behind,
How am I going to find them?
Baa, baa, Compère Bouqui, baa, baa."

Absentmindedly, Bouqui took up the tune:

"They will find you in my pot
With pepper sauce good and hot."

Then he caught himself. "Ha, ha, little kid. That's a beautiful song. Who taught it to you? Teach it to me, no," Bouqui said.

"My maman taught it to me. You haven't heard anything yet."

"No?" Bouqui replied.

"Just be kind enough to release my two front feet. Then you'll see how beautifully I can sing."

"Sure, sure, kindness is my name," Bouqui released the two front feet of the kid. "Nice feet, nice breast for a *calalou* you have there, little kid."

> "Baa, baa, Compère Bouqui, baa, baa
> My maman has left me behind
> My papa has left me behind
> How am I going to find them?
> Baa, baa, Compère Bouqui, baa, baa."

Bouqui took up the tune.

> "They will find you in my pot
> With pepper sauce good and hot."

"That is the most beautiful song I've ever heard, little kid. Sing it again so I can learn it."

"You haven't heard anything yet. I could sing it with more power and more clarity, if you would be good enough to free my two hind legs. My vocal cords will be freer to sing notes as clear as crystal. You'll hear and learn better."

"No? Really? Continue little goat. My ears are stretched to hear you sing."

Bouqui let go of the goat's two hind legs.

Quickly the little kid turned around and gave Bouqui a hard butt, which pitched him over the high cliff. Then the kid took a few leaps and joined the flock.

A good while after the crash, Bouqui came to.

He muttered, "That's what I get for showing understanding and kindness to that nasty goat. I should not have listened to him. Now here I am without goat meat to eat. As my Grand-Mère use to say, 'It's the crab's kind heart that keeps it from having a head. That's it.'

He pulled himself together and went home, disappointed and well bruised.

Lidie et Tina

GLOSSARY

ac	with; native contraction for avec
anneau d 'or	golden ring
bocor	voodoo doctor
calalou	stew
calabash	drinking gourd
cassava	a round sheet of cassava bread
chanteuse	singer
chaudière	iron kettle
cher, chère	dear
cocomacaque	long stick
Colibri	a green, red and blue-feathered bird of the hummingbird family
commère	godmother
compère	godfather
couis	eating gourd
cousin-seeds	seeds covered with sharp pointed thorns
diablesse	she-devil
doucounou	corn meal cake
entamé	well begun
Frê	brother
garçon	boy
grand Frê	elder brother
halfor	straw bag with a long string
hounfort	magic altar
houngan	voodoo doctor
Housi-canzo	one who need not fear fire (African)
Il était une fois	Once upon a time
la queue	kind of fish
lait de chaux	limewater
laissez-moi	leave me alone

Loa	voodoo spirit or god
loup-garou	werewolf
macaque	monkey
machete	agricultural tool, knife-like
macoute	straw sack
marraine	godmother
maté	a beverage made of green leaves
méchant	wicked
mes amis	my friends
metsignin	an herb
mi-mangé	half gone
Neveu	nephew
nganga	witch doctor
Nonc	uncle
ouanga	voodoo, magic
petit	small, young
poupées	dolls
prière	prayer, funeral feast, or memorial celebration
rapadou	round bar of sugar candy, wrapped in a palm husk
tafia	an alcoholic drink
Tantine	aunt
ti-chatte	dear little cat
Tonton	uncle
tout-fini	all gone
vieux	old
zammi mouin	dear friend
zapate	native made sandals
zombi	the walking dead

Les Maîtresses Métissées (Mulatto Women)

ABOUT THE
AUTHOR/ARTIST

Adventurous, independent, creative, multi-talented, and somewhat mysterious are adjectives that have all been used to describe François Turenne des Prés.

Born in 1907 to a middle class Haitian family that owned coffee and sugar plantations, Turenne des Prés always wanted to make his own mark upon the world. At age sixteen, shortly after the death of his father, he left home and travelled through the Caribbean, Central America, and Canada, eventually arriving in the United States.

In his early twenties and in a new country, Turenne des Prés decided to pursue his education. He worked during the day to pay for his studies at Atlanta University, where he majored in his first love, music. Exposure to the Romance languages, English literature, and folklore, however, charted an entirely different course for his life. After the publication of a paper he had written in the style of the twelfth century author Chaucer was warmly received, he was encouraged to write the stories of Haiti, which had been recounted to him by his grandmother, San Naa, and the nursemaid, Ma Bonne. Several of these tales were printed singly over a number of years until eventually he decided to put the Malice and Bouqui stories into one volume called *Children of Yayoute*, published in Haiti in 1949.

Wanting the reader to see the world from which his stories originated, Turenne des Prés illustrated one tale. The process awakened in him what he saw as a natural talent. Although he continued to write, his focus began to shift towards a greater emphasis on the visual arts.

Turenne des Prés met and married a French citizen, Marguerite Reynaud, and with their two sons, Tristan and Josquin, lived in France for twelve years, where he painted and exhibited extensively.

After returning to the United States, the family settled in San Diego, California, where François died in 1990. He left behind over 300 paintings, several unpublished folktales, and one published volume of Haitian folktales, the first to be printed in the English language.

This book is a tribute to his ability to vividly tell the story of Haitian life on paper and canvas.

All works, in alphabetical order, are by François Turenne des Prés.

Carnaval Haitien (Haitian Carnival)
oil on canvas, 25 x 30 in.
Trust of François Turenne des Prés

Une Case dans la Brousse (A Hut in the Jungle)
oil on canvas, 24 x 30 in.
Trust of François Turenne des Prés

Chanson pour une Demi-déesse Blessèe
(Song for a Wounded semi-goddess)
oil on canvas, 48 x 52 in.
Trust of François Turenne des Prés

Conte Vaudouesque (Voodoo Story)
oil on canvas, 36 x 44 in.
Gift to CAAM Foundation

Conversation à Trois (Three Conversing), 1956
oil on masonite, 24 x 20 in.
Gift to CAAM Foundation

Dans une Plage Caraibe
(On the Carribean Seashore), 1956
oil on canvas, 35 x 39 in.
Gift to CAAM Foundation

Deux Bonnes Femmes (Two Good Women)
oil on canvas, 30 x 24 in.
Gift to CAAM Foundation

Les Deux Commères (Two Gossipers)
oil on canvas, 40 x 28 in.
Trust of François Turenne des Prés

Félicité
oil on canvas, 50 x 54 in.
Trust of François Turenne des Prés

Une Femme Assise (Sitting Woman)
oil on canvas, 25 x 30 in.
Trust of François Turenne des Prés

Fille avec Fruits sur la Tête (Girl with Fruit on her Head)
oil on cardboard, 20 x 16 in.
Gift to CAAM Foundation

Haitian Country Scene
oil on canvas, 20 x 24 in.
Gift to CAAM Foundation

Harmonie Champêtre (Country Harmony)
watercolor on paper, 22 x 30 in.
Trust of François Turenne des Prés

Humilité
oil on masonite, 26 x 18 in.
Gift to CAAM Foundation

Jeu sur le Chemin (Game on the Path)
oil on masonite, 20 x 16 in.
Gift to CAAM Foundation

Lidie et Tina, 1957
oil on canvas, 30 x 25 in.
Gift to CAAM Foundation

Les Maîtresses Métissées (Mulato Women)
oil on canvas, 35 x 40 in.
Trust of François Turenne des Prés

Le Marche Haitien (Haitian Market)
watercolor on paper, 21 x 29 in.
Collection of Chantal Creuza Turenne des Prés

Nue—L'Haitienne (Haitian Nude), 1959
oil on canvas, 30 x 24 in.
Gift to CAAM Foundation

Oh, Mauvaise Augure! (Omen!)
oil on board, 30 x 24 in.
Trust of François Turenne des Prés

Paysage Haitien (Haitian Scene)
oil on canvas, 48 x 58 in.
Trust of François Turenne des Prés

Paysage Tropical (Tropical Landscape)
oil on canvas, 24 x 30 in.
Trust of François Turenne des Prés

Présentation au Temple (Offering at the Temple)
watercolor on paper, 18 x 24 in.
Trust of François Turenne des Prés

Le Triage des Grains (The Grain Harvest)
oil on canvas, 50 x 54 in.
Trust of François Turenne des Prés

Voodoo Priestess
oil on board, 30 x 24 in.
Trust of François Turenne des Prés